Essential Rugby

Paragon Publishing Ltd
Paragon House
St Peter's Road
Bournemouth
United Kingdom
BH1 2JS

Tel: +44 (0)1202 299900
Fax: +44 (0)1202 299955
Email: books@paragon.co.uk
http://www.paragon.co.uk

Essential Rugby
© RDT Ltd
© 1999 Paragon Publishing

British Library Cataloguing-in-Publication-Data
A catalogue for this book is available from the British Library

ISBN 1-84179-024-9

All rights reserved. No part of this publication may be reproduced, stored in a retrieval system, or transmitted in any form whatsoever without the written consent of the publishers. This book may not be lent, re-sold hired out or otherwise disposed of by way of trade in any form if binding or cover other than that in which it is published.

While every effort has been made to ensure that the information contained in **Essential Rugby** is accurate, Paragon Publishing Ltd makes no warranty, either expressed or implied, as to its quality, performance, merchantability or fitness for any purpose.

Printed by: Mackays of Chatham, Badger Road, Lordswood, Chatham, Kent

Published by: Paragon Publishing Ltd

Essential Rugby

WRITTEN BY
Neil Armstrong

SNR PRODUCTION EDITOR
Lou Wells

DESIGNED BY
Steven Gotobed

Printed and bound in Great Britainby
Mackays of Chatham

All contents of this book
© Paragon Publishing 1999

Contents

Introduction	07
Section 1 – A Short History of Rugby	08
Section 2 – The Modern Game	28
Section 3 – The Five Nations Tournament	62
Section 4 – Allied Dunbar Premiership and Prominent Players	70
Section 5 – Fact and feats – Odds & Sods	150
A – Z of Rugby	172

Introduction

As all Rugby Union fans prepare to take part as spectators in the World Cup Finals in England and Wales this October 1999, the game itself is stronger and more popular than ever before. The game is older than Association Football and has been adapted into many versions around the world having influence in as far reaching locations as Fiji, Australia, the Middle East and of course New Zealand, land of the All-Blacks, probably the most famous of Rugby Union nations.

Rugby League is also at the height of its popularity, underlining that in general terms 'Rugby' is one of the most watched and most played sports on the planet, and if you take into consideration that Gaelic Football, American Football and many other 'localised' games have derived from the game of rugby, that would make it as popular as soccer on a world scale!

This book is really a guide to the rise and rise of rugby worldwide, and has been written with both the 'real' and existing fan in mind as well as a more general guide for all those people who are going to fall in love with the game over the course of what promises to be an 'unbeatable' World Cup Tournament.

In this Anoraks Guide, you will find a brief history of the game, which has its beginnings way before 1823, the year that is generally regarded as the birth date of Rugby. All the major happenings in the game have been catalogued and recorded here, right through to the modern game and its place in the modern world of Sports.

You will also find a history of the Five-Nations Championship, the oldest and best known international rugby competition in the world. This book also contains a guide to the game at club level in England, all the honours and all the most prominent players are contained within. Finally, for all of you real Rugby Anoraks, the book is packed to the brim with facts, figures and feats stretching right across the history of the game.

I hope you will enjoy the book and keep it for reference in the future as the game of rugby heads into a new millennium, reaching new audiences and fans as it goes.

Neil Armstrong

SECTION 1 – A SHORT HISTORY OF RUGBY

A Short History of Rugby

While playing football at Rugby School, England, one summer's day in 1823, William Webb Ellis, one of hundreds of young 'footballers' playing within the schools grounds, picked up the ball in his hands and ran with it, breaking the established rules of the game. This school ground 'incident' is said to have sparked an interest, leading to the creation of rugby football.

That is the generally accepted story of the beginning of Rugby, but was this the birth of a popular game or was it simply the coming of age rounded up into an interesting yet improbable story?

If some young 'whipper-snapper' had picked up the ball and ran with it at our school, while that lads were engaged in a football match, he would have been beaten to a pulp and would never be allowed near the pitch again! However, not at Rugby School, where Ellis is to this day credited with 'inventing' the game. He is even immortalised at the school with a stone plaque reading:

THIS STONE
COMMEMORATES THE EXPLOIT OF
WILLIAM WEBB ELLIS
WHO WITH A FINE DISREGARD FOR THE RULES OF
FOOTBALL,
AS PLAYED IN HIS TIME,
FIRST TOOK THE BALL IN HIS ARMS AND RAN WITH IT,
THUS ORIGINATING THE DISTINCTIVE FEATURES OF
THE RUGBY GAME
AD 1823

Of course the story is most likely to be untrue, since games involving running with a 'ball' in hand had existed for centuries before that, and in fact the 'School rules' of football at the time most probably included running with the ball in hand, an early feature of soccer since it was created, although not part of the modern game.

So, if you dispute the William Webb Ellis story, where did Rugby Football come from?

Well, the evolution of rugby, closely resembles that of soccer and up until the point when Association Soccer and rugby football became two very different things, the games that had been played for the last 2,000 years had elements of both modern games in their make-ups.

The Romans played a game called 'Herpastum', which involved two sets of players contesting possession of a large ball while trying to throw this ball through the oppositions goal. The game featured a mass maul to gain possession of the ball and team members supporting each other in an attempt to move the ball forward. These features sound very much like rugby mauls and the game featured elements not too dissimilar to a scrummage. These were just some of the features of the game that may have been evolved into rugby football. Other features of the game are said to have evolved into other games over the course of many hundreds of years, including soccer and basketball, the game having begun with a form of 'tip-off'.

Whether the game of Herpastum was the beginning of it all is another matter. It is logical to presume that for many hundreds of years before this Roman game, other games had come and gone and evolved into Herpastum. It is clear though, that the roots of many modern games are buried deep in the past, with many 'local' variations all adding to what had been established to make another and so on... One thing is clear though, the game of rugby football wasn't invented overnight and certainly not by some small boy who had such vision that he single-handedly 'poked-fun' at an already established game and led some 'swash-buckling' rebellion that led to the formation of an independent game, although who knows? He might have had something to do with it!

The probable truth is that most of our modern games have, in some part, evolved over many hundreds of years and we can only look to recent history of indicators, such as games played in the Middle Ages and more recently that have in some way been recorded.

Edward II, Edward III, Henry VIII and Elizabeth I have all been recorded as taking a dim view on many games of violence and mass competition played in the streets, manors and counties of the British Isles that have been collectively referred to as 'football'. These games featured mass brawls with scores of injuries and even fatalities as over-excited men chased around streets after a ball. Even today we see small examples of this type of passion on our football or rugby fields when

SECTION 1 – A SHORT HISTORY OF RUGBY

players seem to get stuck into each another in the 'heat' of competition. Famous examples from history of these types of games were played on Shrove Tuesday, most famously in the streets of Derby and Chester.

These games featured entire villages running after possession of a ball by wrestling each other to the ground and passing the ball to teammates by hand. Other games involved kicking the ball as well. These popular games are certainly steps in the evolution of both soccer and rugby football. Versions of this game were played all over the British Isles and have been recorded in history books in venues such as Corfe Castle in Dorset, Alnwick Castle in Northumberland and of-course Derbyshire, giving rise to the modern term 'Derby'.

If the Rugby School incident did anything for the game of rugby, it established it rather than invented it. From that moment on, the game began to be recognised as a sport, and popularity grew at an astonishing rate.

Establishing The Rules

Cambridge University immediately adopted the game, popularised it and made local rules. In 1843, the first rugby club was formed at Guy's Hospital, London and rugby began to spread.

In 1851, a 'Rugby School Football' was made by William Gilbert. The oval-shaped ball, which was an inflated pig's bladder, gave rugby a true distinction from soccer and the shape of the ball would be retained for evermore. The firm Gilbert's also produced the ball for the 1851 London Exhibition.

In 1854, the sport of rugby reached the Irish shores and the Dublin University club was founded, the first in Ireland. Many Rugby Union clubs started to spring up around the United Kingdom, but it wasn't until 1863 that the first recorded club game took place. Richmond v Blackheath was the tie, and remains as the oldest regular fixture in Rugby Union Football anywhere in the world. Within a few years, Rugby swept across the world, and began to gain popularity, not only in Britain, but in New Zealand, Australia and South Africa. In 1870, the first rugby game in New Zealand was played, all this without officially recognised and consistent rules.

The game grew in stature at area schools and in 1871, ten years after the common rules of soccer were set, the first Rugby Union was founded in London and firm rules of the game were established, although regional rules still continued in some areas, the official game had arrived and further changes to rules and regulations would all be derived from the first Rugby Union rules of 1871. Also in that very same historic year, the first ever international game was held. The participating counties were Scotland and England, the game was played at Raeburn Place in Edinburgh on Monday 27 March 1871. The game was played for fifty minutes each way and Scotland were victorious, winning by a goal and a try to England's try. England did, however, get their revenge in the following year, winning by two goals and two tries to a goal in a return match at the Oval.

Also in 1872 the first rugby club was formed in France. Le Havre, were to start a great French affiliation with the game of Rugby Union Football that would later show France to be one of the Super Powers in World Rugby. But even as early as this in the established game of Union, there were rumblings and arguments, primarily about the status of the game.

In 1877 the number of players allowed on the field of play in international teams reduced from twenty to fifteen and the game began to reach more and more countries. In 1880, Rugby was introduced to Argentina and began to spread across the South American continent while the game in Britain was developing at an astonishing rate especially in Northern England, where many clubs started to raise more concerns about the status of Rugby Football, especially when compared to the professional evolution of Association Football.

Two years before, in 1875, the first rugby matches between England and Ireland took place, with England winning ten and drawing one of their first eleven matches against the Irish. In 1881, the first England versus Wales game took place at Blackheath and England quickly established superiority there as well. The first game was won by such a margin by England that the fixture didn't reoccur until two years later. England went on to win the next four matches against the Welsh.

The game was still developing though, even in the UK. Rules were still be 'updated', formal competitions were still in their infancy. In wasn't until 1886 that Scotland, Wales and Ireland founded the International Rugby Board (IRB). With its headquarters in Dublin, Ireland, the IRB is the World Governing and Law-making body for the Game of Rugby Union.

In 1887, at the meeting of the IRB held in Manchester, under the chairmanship of JS Carrick of Scotland the following resolutions were adopted:

1. That all International Matches must be played under rules approved of

SECTION 1 – A SHORT HISTORY OF RUGBY

by an International Board.//
2. That an International Board be immediately formed under the above Resolution.//
3. That the same International Board shall have absolute and exclusive jurisdiction over all disputes arising in International Matches played under its Rules.//
4. That the Board shall consist of three representatives from each of the Unions, that the Chairman shall be appointed at each Meeting in regular rotation from the different Unions commencing in the order of seniority, and that the Board shall appoint as Honorary Secretary anyone they may think fit.

It wasn't until 1890 that England joined the other home nations within the IRB. This made the foundation considerably stronger and the board began to influence Rugby on the World stage, developing policy as they went along, improving the game and creating solid foundations for the future of International competition.

Playing For Love

Perhaps the most widely known feature of Rugby Union when it was formed and for the next hundred plus years was the amateur status given to the game. This fact has always been at the forefront of Rugby arguments and discussions. As early as 1895, rugby clubs in northern England called for compensation of lost wages for players. Arguments ensued, amateur status was maintained and the result was that The Rugby League was founded and a thirteen-player game with altered rules was created for professionals. A game that was so young in its established life had already come to a head and split into two schools of thought. A situation that would remain.

Rugby Union held out as a strictly amateur sport whereas Rugby League became professional (at least at the highest level). The split was extremely acrimonious; so much so that a painting of a rugby match that had been commissioned had players who defected to league removed. For a hundred years, Rugby Union authorities stuck to their principles and steadfastly refused to permit player payments. It was also against the union rules on amateurism for union players to be involved in any way with league. Even as late as the Seventies it was normal for union players who switched to League to be ostracised and frowned upon by the Union rule-makers.

Rugby Union continued to spread across the globe and competition emerged between countries. In 1897, Rugby was introduced to Japan while in the United States, the game emerged primarily on the West Coast. The lack of precise rules, ambiguities in the game and complexity of the sport pushed many American players away from the game and major changes were invoked. In 1880 the scrum was replaced by a line of scrimmage, drawing emphasis from the free-running characteristic of the game. The game continued to be played with rugby rules until 1905 where the publication of photographs of a harsh game between Sarthmore and Pennsylvania created a stir. President Theodore Roosevelt insisted on reform of the game to lower the brutality with the threat of abolishing the game by edict. In 1906 the forward pass was introduced to the United States game. The rules of rugby died and the game of American football was born.

Although a handful of clubs remained in the United States, rugby did not re-emerge until the Sixties. College campuses turned to the sport because it was one where many could play and escape the rigid discipline and professionalism inherent in college football. Minimal costs, constant action and the opportunity for frequent play with a primary emphasis on fun also attracted many. The number of clubs grew from about eighty to over a thousand between 1964 and 1980. The United States of America Rugby Football Union (USARFU) was formed in 1975, creating added recognition and a measure of organisation.

Global Recognition

The turn of the century was celebrated with the 1900 Olympic games in Paris, Rugby Union appearing for the first time with the host nation taking the Gold medal. Only three teams took part in the competition; France, Germany and Britain. France took the gold, winning 27-17 against Germany, who were awarded the silver medal. Britain lost 27-8 to France in the only other match, and were awarded the bronze.

The next 'great event' came some years later in 1905, when New Zealand toured the British Isles, Canada and the USA. This was not only a concept that would promote rugby around the world and in many ways bring the game to a further level, it was also a very successful tour for the All-Blacks who started their grasp on the world game, a grasp which they still hold very close to their chests approaching a hundred years later! The touring New Zealanders

SECTION 1 – A SHORT HISTORY OF RUGBY

brought to Europe and North America a style of play that was fast, exciting and highly technical. Their philosophy was that passing the ball was the single most important aspect of the game, and that they did to great effect. Their captain Dave Gallaher and their vice-captain Billy Stead were great authorities on the game and in fact had co-written a book together entitled *The Complete Rugby Football*, which described in detail all tactical and technical aspects of the game. It underlined that passing, team movement, team organisation and planning were crucial to winning a rugby match, and on this tour they certainly practised what they preached. In 1905, the All-Blacks had a full itinerary of planned and pre-arranged moves which they engaged with great skill, flair and accuracy. Some of the tactics even included splitting the line-out and throwing the ball into the gap that had been created. This would then allow the blindside winger to run forwards, take the ball in his stride and take the attack to the opposition. On the tour the All-Blacks scored 33 tries directly from line-outs, an innovation which turned the normal 'throw-in to re-start' approach, into an instant attacking move.

Gallaher and Stead masterminded these movements of 'planned deception' and employed them to great success. The All-Blacks had developed their very own, unique style of play, and echoes of these early days can still be found in the modern day set-up. They put specialists in certain areas, something that had never been done before. Their forward line was tough and strong with great technical abilities and strength. They seldom lost a scrummage in this tour and even if the opposition hooked the ball from their put-in, the eighth forward, who was then called a wing-forward, would employ spoiling tactics, using quick feet and unhindered excess, to promptly tackle and snatch the ball back. The 1905 All-Blacks were a well oiled unit with players in specialist positions and formations, all of which had their very own specialist 'ruses' to foil the opposition.

The New Zealand tourists worked hard on the training pitch and introduced 'code-word' systems for their pre-arranged patterns of play, so that tactics could be instantly adjusted on the pitch and all their players would know what was going on. They established a workable, passing line behind the scrum, which moved forwards at pace, passing as they went and they mastered the 'ruck' or 'lose-scrummage' as it was then known, by staying on their feet, pushing, turning and working the ball, rather than the well-practised and well-used British tactic of simply 'falling' on the ball and hope that the referee gives a scrummage. This touring party was unique and innovative in every way. They introduced 'miss-moves', missing out backs in the line to move the ball out quicker. They engaged false or 'dummy' runners in free-kick situations and they kicked the ball only when absolutely necessary, often to get the ball into touch, thus giving them a chance to break from the line-out.

They brought an intelligence into the game and analysed their game scientifically and statistically; at this point in time, that common reaction to the ball going over the side-line was to opt for a scrummage further in field! The New Zealanders changed all that and they would hold the advantage over most teams in the world for a very long time to come. The All-Black tour performances had awakened many countries and club teams to these 'new techniques', and they led the way into rugby becoming much more of a spectacle to take part in of to watch. Their tour had been so successful (they shone in Canada, USA and France) that by the time they were returning home from the USA, a similar tour was being planned by the South Africans.

The 1906 South Africans were almost as successful as the All-Blacks had been the year before. They beat Ireland and Wales, drew with England and were only beaten in a close match by Scotland and in the final match of their tour against Cardiff. Although they were not as cultured or skilled as the All-Blacks, they were somewhat organised and played very well throughout their tour. The performances of the Springboks legendary Centre Jaapie Krige were especially notable. His pace and footwork were untouchable and the backs which he lead were lean and fit. This was a glimpse of another world rugby superpower shaping up.

The Demise Of The British Game

In 1908 the first Australian tour of England and Wales came, with the Australians winning the rugby competition in the London Olympics, employing many of the movements that had been introduced to the world by the All-Blacks and more variations of their own. In this Olympic challenge though, only two teams entered; Britain, the hosts, and Australia. Just one match was played, a straight final, won by Australia 32-3. Had the New Zealanders attended the games it might well have been a different story, but one thing would have remained obvious. Britain was falling behind in the game of Rugby Union. The

SECTION 1 – A SHORT HISTORY OF RUGBY

rest of the world were training harder, had more technical ability and it would seem, much more of a will to win. This is a problem that has often been levelled at British soccer over the years, and to some extent it was as true for the rugby as it is for the soccer!

In 1912, the Springboks returned to the Britain and this time the South Africans showed no rough edges. They proceeded to defeat all in their path. The Scots were swept aside 16-0, the Irish were thrashed 38-0, they defeated a strong Welsh team 3-0 and they completed there whistle-stop winning strike with the 9-3 defeat of England, who were the only team to score points against them on the tour. Rugby Union was growing up all around the world. The performances of the All-Blacks and the Springboks had shown the world that they were not only superb exponents of the game, but that the game itself had developed into a tremendous sport to watch or to play. Rugby had well and truly arrived and the game was beginning to spread into new territories. In 1914, rugby was introduced to Romania, just as the First World War began to take its toll and just as in Association Football, rugby found it hard to progress forwards during this period.

In 1912, the United States of America took part in their first international match against Australia and the following year saw them take on New Zealand. These were small beginnings for the American game, but their most famous exploit in rugby union was just a few short years away.

By 1920, the world had recovered from the First World War and sport was once again the focus. It was another Olympic year, the venue Antwerp and again only two teams entered. This time it was the USA and France. The USA causing a shock by winning the only match 8-0 to take the gold medal. This was the very first time that the USA had played against France in an international match.

Just four years later in 1924, Paris was the venue for the fourth and final appearance of Rugby Union in the Olympic games. Three teams entered – France, USA and Romania – each country played two games. Both France and USA beat Romania, who were awarded the bronze medal. France won 59-3, scoring thirteen tries including four by the fine French winger, Adolphe Jaureguy.

The USA then defeated Romania 39-0. The final was played at the Columbus stadium, Paris on 18 May 1924 and the USA took the gold with a 17-3 victory before over thirty thousand spectators.

The Americans, from Stanford University, scored five tries (Farrish (two), Patrick, Rogers and Manelli), with a conversion from Doe. Gallau scored the lone French try. The match finished in uproar, when Gideon Nelson, one of the reserves, was flattened during a fight by a walking stick. The American anthem was jeered, and rugby ceased to be an event at the Olympics.

A Laboured Progression

Over the next two decades, the game grew and grew. The IRB memberships and associated memberships were expanding and rugby was being introduced in more and more places. In 1927 the very first international match between France and Germany took place. This was followed soon after by the formation of the British Lions, a team drawn from all corners of Britain in order to give teams like Australia, South Africa and New Zealand more competition.

It was in 1931 that a regular international challenge tournament named the Bledisloe Cup between New Zealand and Australia was founded. Two years later, Australia toured South Africa and took part in the first international match between the two great nations.

Rugby was being introduced into other countries at a steady rate. Italy embraced the game and started to play against other nations by 1937, when they took on France. The French at this time were domestically in turmoil, with the old question of 'professionalism' creeping in again. The Federation Française de Rugby, had fallen out with the IRB and the Four Home Unions over payments to players, other than out-of-pocket expenses. This, however, did get sorted out but the reasons for the sudden change of heart by the French and wanting to remain with the world game was probably due more to the impending War in Europe.

The Second World War, again halted the progression of rugby, especially in Europe, with the suspension of many of the tournaments that had now become fully installed into the sporting calendar, such as the Five Nations. However, many of the top rugby players of the time were still able to compete by playing for the services that they had found themselves in. During the war, many renown players would take part, thus keeping the interest in the game, keeping fit and keeping the game going through difficult times. Teams were formed from a mix of League and Union players and 'internationals' of sorts were played. Once a New Zealand division took on South Africa in the middle of the desert.

SECTION 1 – A SHORT HISTORY OF RUGBY

After the war, the first competitive rugby was still part of this Inter-services system. Commanding officer of the New Zealand division, General Freiburg, decided that it would be a good idea to form a team from the New Zealand army to travel to Great Britain when the Second World War ended in 1945. This team was captained by Charlie Saxton, an All-Black scrum-half and the rest of the team was selected from the entire New Zealand forces, who were stationed in Europe, Asia and Africa.

After training sessions in Italy and trial sessions in Austria, the 'Kiwis' were ready to tour with a team that was every bit as good as the pre-war All-Blacks, although Saxton was the only All-Black on the team. The tour was a great success and the New Zealanders more or less cleaned up on the tour, sweeping most of the team aside. This whetted the appetite for the return of international competition and in 1946 the Five Nations Championship resumed.

Two years later, Australia, New Zealand and South Africa officially joined the IRB and the Australian Rugby Football Union was founded. Now rugby began to develop at a quick pace again, as countries tried to make up for the lost time in the two recent World Wars.

In 1947, the first test match between Scotland and Australia took place, and on the same tour the first Ireland versus Australia fixture occurred. These were heady, feel-good days and that was reflected on the rugby pitch. Teams travelled around Europe taking each other on. France was a very popular venue, especially by teams from the British Isles, as rationing had ended in France, while it remained back home. The Australians too, couldn't get enough of Europe, as there were plenty of willing teams to play. In 1948, France took on the Australian side for the first time, domestic leagues were completely up to speed across Europe and the Five Nations Championship was again attracting large crowds and plenty of interest.

The Forties ended with Argentina joining the touring circuit and the Fifties were to introduce the likes of Fiji and Czechoslovakia to the world game and consolidate South Africa as the world's number one rugby nation. In the 1949 series between South Africa and the All-Blacks, the Springboks out-played and out-classed the New Zealanders, but although South Africa was moving further ahead of the rest of the world, it didn't mean that it was the end of the All-Blacks, who promptly displayed the fact that although they were behind South Africa, they were still well ahead of everyone else. When the British Lions toured New Zealand in 1950, the All-Blacks swept the series 3-0 after the first test had been drawn. The British forwards who played on that tour all confessed afterwards that it was a humbling experience. On a global scale, it was clear South Africa and New Zealand were the major forces in world rugby, and all in the British Isles were falling behind.

Scotland, who had won the Calcutta Cup in 1950, were, at the point, only a couple of wins behind England in all the matches that they had played since 1871. Scotland were considered a strong nation in world terms, until they met the Springboks, losing 44-0. From that day on, Scotland lost their way, losing 17 matches in succession and not winning again until 1955.

Worldwide Status

On the world stage, the game was still evolving at a tremendous pace, but it was seen in 1958, that a code of practice, pertaining to players and officials need to be nailed down. 'Rules as to Professionalism' were then included in the Laws of the Game, although Rugby Union was far from turning completely professional, even with constant pressure from all corners of the globe.

In 1959, France (perhaps the greatest protagonists in the 'Professional' debate) won the Five Nations outright for the first time ever. This sent a clear and concise message to British rugby. The Home nations were clearly being beaten at their own game in a tournament that had seen total domination by the home nations since it became the 'Five Nations'.

The turn of the Sixties did however see some sort of up-turn in fortunes. The British Lions toured New Zealand again and played extremely well. In a tremendous tour by probably the best set of British players ever to be assembled, they out-played the All-Blacks in most departments, yet still lost the tour 3-1, a result that many found hard to believe considering what happen on the tour. In the first match, the lions scored four tries to New Zealand's zero, but still ended up losing the match 18-17! The second test was as close but again went to the home side. The Lions well beaten in the third test in convincing style, but took the final test, to recover some dignity and collect some justice for their wonderful tour performances. Most of the touring party who went to New Zealand in 1959, still can't believe they lost the tour 3-1, when they should have won it by the same margin!

The Sixties also saw a real surge in touring. More and more countries were entering the competition, more club sides were taking tours abroad

SECTION 1 – A SHORT HISTORY OF RUGBY

and the game continued to grow at an astonishing pace. Oxford and Cambridge Universities had already toured Argentina and Japan by 1960 and with the development of air travel, more teams took to the skies to try their fortune on foreign fields. Pressure was put on the Home nations by South Africa, who wanted more international challenges and so the 'short tour' evolved. Scotland travelled to South Africa in 1960, Ireland followed in the following year, Wales toured in 1964 and England completed the cycle in 1972. This encouraged many more tours than ever before. England went to New Zealand in 1963 and 1973, Wales, Scotland and Ireland followed suit and the Home nations all travelled to Australia within the decade.

In 1965 Argentina toured South Africa, France supported Argentina's growing world importance by taking short tours there and in 1969 the First Asian Championship was born, thus bringing competition to yet another region. In 1971, the RFU Centenary Congress was attended by representatives from forty-three rugby playing countries, underlining just how far the game had come since the end of the Second World War. The Sixties and early Seventies saw the major teams visiting each others shores in regular fashion and talk of a 'Rugby World Cup' was beginning to circulate.

Unfortunately, this massive undertaking wouldn't happen for some years to come, but many pundits and ardent fans of the game seem to drool at the mouth with thought of what might of happened if such a competition had been organised within this pioneering period.

A Question Of Money

Of course, with all these touring, International tests, club tours and short tours taking place, the financial pressures on Rugby Union were immense, yet the game refused to be dragged into a professional scenario, where sponsorship and business could help ease the pressures. As if to 'stamp-out' the unsettling rumblings within the ranks, 'Amateur Regulations' replaced the 'Rules as to Professionalism', they also included in the Laws of the Game in 1974. This did little to further the advancement of Rugby Union to a professional level and did even less to quell the opinions that such an event had to happen, sooner rather than later.

In 1974 though, positive things were happening. The world game had grown and flourished, building up momentum with the immense success of the 1967 All-Blacks, who had help to bring Rugby Union to new countries, cultures and people. The World game was about to bust of the banks of expectations and truly arrive. Rugby was about to embark on a revolution no less!

In South Africa, Springbok rugby was destroyed by a British Lions team playing a game of scrummaging and kicking which embraced organised violence, which was totally alien to the British heritage of back-play. This caused a sensation of sorts. The performances by the Lions in South Africa were forcing the main nations to re-evaluate the way that they played. In New Zealand, they threw out this 'new' style of play and put a great deal of effort into evolving their backs' play. In Australia, they began to work on their strategies, toughening up their forward play to match the Lions display, while in France, the hard hitting success of the Beziers club, who had adopted many 'new' techniques, forced the national side to look again at the way they were teaching, coaching, training, developing and playing Rugby Union.

The 1974 'revolution' in actual fact forced seven major nations to change their 'traditional' style of play and choose to move in another direction. This major 'reshuffling' changed the face of world rugby. South Africa, who for many years had been the pick of the international teams, finished the year in tatters. The British Lions beat them 3-0 in the test series (one match being drawn) and they were no longer the team that had held the number one spot in the world rankings almost consistently for the last seventy years.

How could this have happened though? Well, the reasons are many, but perhaps the main reason had been that South Africa had a based team that saw only minor personnel changes with every tour. Rarely did more that three to four players turn around in their international set-up between tours, which is fine if you are playing. However, over the first four years of the Seventies South Africa had only played a short tour of Australia and one match against England. They had 'lost-touch' with the fast-paced evolution of the game and that had led to their fall from grace. The tide had turned, and over the next few years, the play, pace, style and competition of Rugby Union would carve a different path into the future. More teams started to play and train more intensely. More countries began to come through and play good international rugby and more players would be devoting a lot more to time to the game – almost like 'professionals' you might say!

The late Seventies saw the First Caribbean championship of Rugby Union in 1977. A year later saw the significant country of France, finally

SECTION 1 – A SHORT HISTORY OF RUGBY

joining the IRB and the 'revolution' of 1974 was beginning to settle down and countries playing styles were being ironed out. The South Africans bounced back from their British Lions' humiliation by defeating the All-Blacks in a test series. Argentina showed a marked improvement on their tours, especially their British tour of 1976.

Wales and France both had their turns at the top of International Rugby, but neither could muster enough to preserve their status. Scotland had an up and down decade, while the English and the Irish had to be content with their players involvement in the Lions set-up when it came to notable successes, but even that wasn't to last, and by the beginning of the Eighties the British Lions had once again fallen behind in the race for world dominance.

Lack Of Talent During The First World Cup

At grass-roots level, the early Eighties saw a slight decline in good young talent coming through the ranks. This was especially evident in England, where every young boy simply wanted to play soccer and the world of Rugby Union didn't seem as inspirational as it had before. However, the Eighties were a time of new emerging countries and new international fixtures on the calendar and the fruition of the World Cup, so it would seem that Rugby Union only went 'out of fashion' for a short time in the UK.

In 1981 Romania started to emerge into the international scene, playing the likes of Scotland and New Zealand for the first time. The USA were also interested in Rugby Union again, which saw their national side playing a fixture against South Africa on a mini-tour and later in the Eighties saw some strange cross-over challenges, like American Football teams playing British clubs at Union and Rugby League, as well as the reverse. Argentina continued to quietly impress in the early Eighties as did other new teams such as Fiji, Western Samoa, Zimbabwe, Korea and Tonga.

In 1986, the Centenary meeting of the IRB took place, with representatives from a total of seventy-six countries in attendance. The main topic of conversation was the well-overdue World Cup, which was arranged for its inaugural appearance in 1987.

Sixteen Unions (by invitation) took part in first Rugby World Cup held in Australia and New Zealand, but the first Rugby World Cup, was not without its critics. Many people felt that a Rugby World Cup was not a feasible option given the fact that there were not sixteen nations of similar playing standards. This view seemed to be prophetic as New Zealand hammered Italy 70-6 in the opening match. The tournament progressed through its group stages with few upsets and the quarter-final line-up was unsurprising. All of the Five Nations were there along with New Zealand and Australia, with Fiji filling the last remaining place. South Africa's political situation excluded them from the tournament, as it did from many top international rugby games, a fact that only changed as South Africa as a nation changed politically.

The knock-out stage was notable for England's defeat at the hands of the Welsh in the quarter-finals, losing 3-16 in Brisbane. Wales' reward was a semi-final match against New Zealand and they had no answer for the power of the All-Blacks, losing 6-49. The other semi-final was a titanic clash in which France, led by Serge Blanco, overcame favourites Australia 30-22. The final was held at Eden Park, Auckland and saw the hosts New Zealand, having amassed 298 points in six matches, defeat France 29-9 to lift the Webb Ellis trophy.

On the whole the first World Cup was successful, although the South Africans weren't there and the 'predictable' nature of the tournament proved some of the critics right, it was nevertheless and important competition to get under way, and the very fact that there was now to be a regular international tournament would spur on the 'lesser teams' and eventually the World Cup would become much more competitive.

Rugby Moves Forward

In 1989, the modern development of the world game took another great step in the right direction. The second international meeting of IRB Member Unions took place, at which an extended membership of the Board was created. An enlarged Executive Council was formed to include Argentina, Canada, Italy and Japan and a date for the next World Cup was settled upon.

In 1990, the first meeting of the new Executive Council (twelve nations) of the Board took place in London. Which was followed by the second World Cup held in the UK, Ireland and France in 1991.

Over thirty teams were involved in the preliminary rounds as the tournament came to the Northern Hemisphere. Organised by the Five Nations Championship, the tournament still only had sixteen teams. This time all Unions in the IRFB membership were invited to enter qualifying

SECTION 1 – A SHORT HISTORY OF RUGBY

rounds. The eight quarter-finalists of 1987 qualified directly for the Tournament while thirty-two other nations competed for the remaining eight places.

Australia were installed as the pre-tournament favourites with New Zealand close behind in the betting stakes. The tournament kicked off with a poor match between England and New Zealand at Twickenham which the Kiwis won 12-18. The shock of the tournament came as Wales crashed 13-16 against the lowly Western Samoans in front of a capacity Cardiff Arms Park crowd. This defeat was followed by a thrashing by Australia six days later which consigned them to an early exit.

The semi-final stage pitted Scotland against England and New Zealand against Australia, the two teams that most regarded as the best in the World Cup. South Africa were still yet to return from their sporting isolation. England secured the first final berth after they survived a hard-fought game against Scotland at Murrayfield in which Gavin Hastings missed an easy penalty to let England off the hook.

The following day, Australia with the explosive talent of David Campese, ended New Zealand's hopes of retaining the trophy with a 16-6 victory. The 1991 Rugby World Cup final at Twickenham again failed to provide a classic match of rugby with Australia defeating England 12-6. However, the tournament had now firmly established itself as one of the top global sporting events.

The success of the World Cup was now leading to other competition innovations. In 1993, twenty-four nations took part in the inaugural Rugby World Cup Sevens held at Murrayfield in Edinburgh, Scotland being the birthplace of this abbreviated version of the Game. England defeated Australia in the final. Then 1994 saw the second General Meeting of the Board held in Vancouver, Canada. The Bahamas and Botswana become Members of the IRB in a meeting which saw sixty-five Unions and Regional Associations in membership.

The following year was another World Cup year, a tournament that would out-shine the previous two competitions by some considerable way. By 1995 the Rugby World Cup had established itself as the fourth largest sporting event in the world, and the bandwagon rolled into South Africa just three years after they had been re-admitted to the rugby community.

In the opening match the Springboks beat Australia 27-18, setting a trend for the remainder of the tournament. The Pool stage had some memorable moments and performances, not least that of Gavin Hastings who scored an incredible forty-four individual points against the Ivory

Coast and followed it up with another 31 against Tonga. This took him to 198 points in the World Cup, surpassing Grant Fox's record of 170. However, the Pool stage was also marred by a serious injury to the Ivory Coast winger Max Brito who was paralysed during a game against Tonga.

Despite this tragedy, the tournament continued and in the meantime a superstar was being born in the form of the massive New Zealand winger Jonah Lomu. Lomu was the centre of attention, steam-rolling his way through sides including England in the semi-finals. England, having beaten Australia with an injury-time drop goal from Rob Andrew, were unable to handle the power of Lomu and the All Blacks, going down 29-45.

In the final the New Zealand side faced the hosts South Africa, who had edged out France in torrential rain in the other semi-final, in front of sixty0three thousand fans in Johannesburg. In a tight match neither side could establish a lead and remained locked at 9-9 after eighty minutes, forcing the game into extra-time. The match was finally settled when the Springbok fly-half Joel Stransky struck a winning drop-goal to claim the trophy for South Africa.

An incredible tournament had reached a massive worldwide audience and had been a real spectacle, well hosted by the eventual winners, 1995 would be remembered as a great year in Rugby Union history not just because of this tournament, but also because of other happenings at a administrational level.

The IRB joined the Olympic Movement as the International Federation for Rugby Union Football, their mission, to re-instate Rugby Union as an Olympic sport. In the Annual Meeting of the Executive Council held in Bristol, UK, the Cook Islands and Zambia become Members of the IRB, taking the total up to sixty-seven Unions in membership. In a special Meeting of the Council in Paris, the 'Regulations Relating to Amateurism' are repealed and replaced by 'Regulations Relating to the Game'.

In August 1995, the biggest innovation to hit Rugby union in its history took place. In the face of widespread abuses (in the form of under the table payments, player trust funds and so on) and pressure from the top players who were being expected to put in many hours of training in an era of increasing media interest in the game, the IRFB finally relinquished and Rugby Union became fully professional at all levels.

Despite their common origins and the fact that both games are now professional, Rugby Union and Rugby League have evolved so far apart that they are best regarded as different sports, although Union stars are sometimes sought out by league scouts and league stars are now

SECTION 1 – A SHORT HISTORY OF RUGBY

occasionally making the transition to Rugby Union. This 'linking' of the two rugby schools of thought, by giving them both a 'level playing field', has not only improved Rugby Union, but has also help Rugby League. Media coverage, and a growing spectator base for both sports, now means that rugby in general is a truly global sport, followed by millions around the world. There are still fanatics who only watch one rugby or the other, but generally there are many more opportunities and cross-overs now, that are enriching the game. Rugby Union continues to grow and is now played in over eighty countries worldwide. The rules of rugby continue to evolve and amateurism remains as dominant characteristic, but a new 'professionalism' is now being recognised, and the game is much better for it.

It was 1996 that saw the first full year of the new 'professional game'. The Third General Meeting of the Board held in Rome, granted memberships of Italy, Slovenia, St Lucia, Bosnia & Herzegovina and Jamaica to the IRB. The count going up to seventy-five Unions and Regional Associations in membership.

Also in 1996, the Laws of the Game changed to allow for up to five tactical substitutions to be made from a maximum of six players named as replacements. The first of one hundred and thirty-eight games involving sixty-six Unions played in the qualifying rounds for the 1999 Rugby World Cup began and the Qualifying tournaments for the 1997 Sevens Rugby World Cup, in Hong Kong began. The Qualifying involving forty-eight Countries, with sixteen qualifying, staged in Lisbon, Portugal, Dubai and United Arab Emirates.

SECTION 2 – THE MODERN GAME

The Modern Game

International Rugby Union currently revolves around a cycle building towards the World Cup, which is staged in a different country every four years, in the same way that the Soccer World Cup is organised. En route to this four yearly 'festival of rugby' there are annual matches and long standing fixtures between neighbouring countries. There are also tours of one (or several) international countries by another. Currently France, Scotland, England, Ireland and Wales play each other in an annual 'tournament' called the Five Nations Championship. All sides play each other on various Saturdays between January and March.

Another major international competition is the Bledisloe Cup which is often played on a knife edge between Australia and New Zealand. The format of this changes from year to year – sometimes it is decided in a one-off test match, and sometimes a series of games decides the outcome of the competition. This contest was augmented in 1996 by a contest between New Zealand, South Africa and Australia which has become an annual event.

There is also a European championship (the FIRA Championship) which is normally dominated by France. There is also an annual game between Canada and the USA in a North American Championship match and an annual competition between Fiji, Tonga and Western Samoa for the South Pacific championship.

In 1996 an eight-nation Pan Pacific series was held involving Samoa, Tonga, Fiji, USA, Canada, Argentina, Japan and Hong Kong. This is also now an annual event. Many of the local internationals between the 'lesser' rugby nations have been included into the World Cup qualifying competitions.

Most countries also have their own internal competitions and national championships. Some also join together to play matches between their various sides. A good example of this is the current Super 10 which involves provincial sides from New Zealand, South Africa and Australia along with the South Pacific Champion (currently Tonga). Another example of international co-operation might be the recent establishment of an inter provincial/district competition involving sides from Scotland and Ireland.

Who's In Charge?

The game is controlled at local level by Rugby Unions which are normally organised on national boundaries, though Northern Ireland and Eire play under the auspices of one union and some US clubs near the border play in Canadian unions.

The governing body for rugby is the International Rugby Football Board (IRFB) commonly referred to as the IRB, founded in 1886. The IRB is responsible for deciding international fixtures, revising the laws of the game and other general matters related to rugby such as amateur status of players. The International Rugby Board, with its headquarters in Dublin, Ireland, was founded in 1886 and typically meets twice per year (normally about March and October). Rugby is played in more than a hundred countries and the IRB membership currently encompasses eighty-three national Unions and one Regional Association, the Paris-based Federation Internationale de Rugby Amateur (FIRA).

The historical membership has expanded enormously in recent times and encompasses all regions, races and people of the world. China became a member in January, 1997. Since then the Cayman Islands, Kazakhstan, Uganda, Madagascar, Monaco, Swaziland, Guam and Venezuela have been admitted to membership.

The Executive Council of the IRB, which meets twice a year, has a membership of twenty-two with two seats held by each of the eight foundation Unions – Scotland, Ireland, Wales, England, Australia, New Zealand, South Africa and France. Argentina, Canada, Italy and Japan – each have one seat on the Council as does FIRA. The full membership meets at a General Meeting, currently convened every two years, the most recent in Buenos Aires in April 1999. Regional meetings are held at regular intervals. The day-to-day business of the IRB is carried out by a 15-strong professional staff who have been located in Dublin since September, 1996.

The objectives and functions of the Board include:
- Promoting, fostering, developing, extending and governing the Game.
- Framing and interpreting the Bye-laws, the Regulations and the Laws of the Game.
- Deciding and/or settling all matters relating to or arising out of the playing or the proposed playing of the Game or a match or between two or more Unions relating to the application of the Bye Laws and Regulations.
- Regulating and co-ordinating arrangements to ensure there is a fair and

SECTION 2 – THE MODERN GAME

equitable programme of matches, tours and tournaments for Senior National Representative teams of all Council Unions.
- Controlling all other matters of an international character that affects the Game.

Increasing Popularity

Until August, 1995 it was an amateur sport. At that point, the Executive Council, recognising rugby's growing pressures as in other high profile sports, its popularity and its ever-increasing commercial value, declared the game 'open'. This meant that, for the first time, players could be remunerated and had the opportunity, if good enough, to become full-time professionals. Children as young as five or six greatly enjoy rugby through non-contact versions of the game. Women's rugby is one of the fastest-growing aspects of the sport while many men continue to play on well into their fifties and sixties, and beyond.

It is played both as a fifteen-a-side game, and also as very popular seven-a-side. Other lesser played versions are ten-a-side and touch rugby, where no tackling is allowed, an established variation and suitable for mixed teams.

The Four Major World Tournaments of The IRB:

The IRB's Rugby World Cup (RWC) one of the world's top five sporting competitions on a list headed by the Olympics and the World Cup of Soccer, was first staged in New Zealand and Australia in 1987. Subsequent tournaments were held in the United Kingdom and France, in 1991, and in South Africa, in 1995. In each case sixteen teams contested the final rounds after qualifying matches involving all the other IRB member Unions over a two-year period.

The winners of the Cup and therefore World Champions have been, New Zealand (1987), Australia (1991) and South Africa (1995). These three nations will all be wanting to claim the 1999 title and are certain to be the favourites to do so.

In 1999, the fourth Rugby World Cup will be hosted by England and Wales with an expanded entry of twenty teams, qualifying through one hundred and thirty-three matches world wide from an original entry of sixty-five Unions. The RWC 1999 Final will be played at the new Millennium Stadium, Cardiff, on 6 November to conclude a forty-one-game, eighteen-venue tournament in Wales, England, Scotland, Ireland and France. The semi-finals will be staged in London with the quarter-finals in Cardiff, Paris, Edinburgh and Dublin.

It is expected that the 1999 tournament will attract over one and a half million spectators with a world wide television audience of over three billion. The estimated gross commercial revenue is $US 105million compared to $US 5.3 in 1987. The 2003 Rugby World Cup will be hosted by Australia with support from New Zealand.

The IRB also holds two other Rugby World Cup tournaments on a four-year cycle. The RWC Sevens is worldwide and involves an even greater number of countries. The first was played in 1993, while the second was in Hong Kong in 1997. Twenty-four teams took part in each of the finals. For 1997, more than seventy countries were involved in qualifying tournaments in Lisbon, Dubai and Punta del Este. The next Rugby World Cup Sevens will be held in Argentina in 2001.

The first Women's Rugby World Cup was held in Edinburgh, in 1991, with the second tournament in Cardiff, in 1994, with USA and England the respective winners. The 1998 Women's Rugby World Cup was hosted by The Netherlands in Amsterdam, and was won by New Zealand. This was the first time the IRB took over the organisation and was directly involved in funding for this event. England, Italy and the USA have expressed interest in hosting WRWC 2002.

The IRB also supports the annual IRB/FIRA World Youth Championship, a very popular Under-nineteen competition that will bring thirty-two countries to Wales in the week before Easter, 1999. Ireland are the defending champions at this level, winning the event for the first time in France, in 1998. Previous recent winners include France and Argentina.

The IRB places great emphasis on the value of competition as a means of raising playing standards and, starting in 1999, plans a significant investment in regional tournaments, among them the Pacific Rim Championship. This investment will enable the three leading South Pacific Islands, Samoa, Fiji and Tonga, to enter into regular annual competition with Canada, Hong Kong, USA and Japan, the original Pacific Rim competing Unions since 1996.

Raising The Game's Profile

Over the last four years, using revenues generated by Rugby World Cup, the IRB has provided development grants of more than £16 million to rugby-playing countries around the world. Funds are allocated to this

SECTION 2 – THE MODERN GAME

programme through a trust, and are used to support coaching competitions, development programmes and other activities that will lead on to greater participation and improved playing standards.

A new IRB teaching aid, 'Play the Game', which is an instructional video and illustrated manual has been translated into many languages, English, French, German, Spanish Mandarin Chinese, Welsh and soon will be in Italian and Japanese. Copies are being provided to all Unions in membership.

The Play the Game programme, which represents an investment about £300,000, is designed to assist teachers and coaches of young people, both boys and girls, with no previous rugby experience.

Rugby is also a proud member of the family of world sports and of the IOC. Full International Olympic Committee (IOC) status was confirmed in September, 1997 and an application is under consideration for rugby's inclusion as a participating sport at the 2004 Olympics.

Rugby made its Olympic debut in 1900 and the USA, Gold Medal Winners in 1924, have been Olympic Champions ever since. That's because rugby was discontinued as an Olympic sport after 1924. Rugby was a first time medal sport at the 1998 Commonwealth Games, in Kuala Lumpur, where New Zealand defeated Fiji in the Final. This three-day event drew entries from eighteen Commonwealth countries and a capacity crowd for the final day's play. Rugby has also been invited to the 2001 World Games in Akita, Japan.

Internationally there are many nations who are just in their infancy on the world rugby scene and many that are well established. Apart from the World Cup winners of New Zealand, Australia and South Africa, that are many teams that, given the right circumstances, could be the next World Champions. England, France, Scotland, Ireland and official hosts Wales are collectively known as the Five Nations, and all go into the 1999 competition, confident that they could provide the fourth World Champions. There are twenty teams competing in the finals but over sixty teams who have been involved in the qualification for these and the past competitions.

Rugby World Cup Nation By Nation All-Time Competition Records

Below is a round-up of all the nations who have been a part of the 1999 World Cup qualification, with details on there competition pedigree. Most of the teams below have never qualified for the final stages, and on them you will find their all-time record in the qualification rounds. For those who have been good enough to compete at the highest level, you will also find there all-time record in the World Cup Final Stages up until the 1999 Championship which begins in October 1999.

ANDORRA
Final Tournaments:
Andorra has not managed to qualify in any of the RWC Final Tournaments.

Qualifying Rounds:
Biggest win   54-24 v Lithuania 1996
Biggest defeat   3-62 v Spain 1997
All-time

Played	Won	Drawn	Lost	Points for	Points against
10	5	0	5	187	295

ARABIAN GULF
Final Tournaments:
Arabian Gulf has not qualified for any of the RWC Final Tournaments.

Qualifying Rounds:
Biggest win   53-13 v Botswana 1997
Biggest defeat   20-64 v Namibia 1997
All-time

Played	Won	Drawn	Lost	Points for	Points against
7	3	0	4	191	229

SECTION 2 – THE MODERN GAME

ARGENTINA
Final Tournaments:
Argentina has competed in all final tournaments since 1987.

Biggest win	25-16 v Italy 1987
Biggest defeat	15-46 New Zealand 1987

All-time

Played	Won	Drawn	Lost	Points for	Points against
9	1	0	8	156	260

Qualifying Rounds:

Biggest win	70-7 v Chile 1995
Biggest defeat	9-15 v Canada 1991

All-time

Played	Won	Drawn	Lost	Points for	Points against
12	10	0	2	402	151

AUSTRALIA
Final Tournaments:
Australia have qualified for the first three RWC Tournaments without having to play anyone

Biggest win	47-12 v USA 1987
Biggest defeat	24-30 v France 1987

All-time

Played	Won	Drawn	Lost	Points for	Points against
16	12	0	4	421	229

Qualifying Rounds

Biggest win	74-0 v Tonga 1999
Biggest defeat	None

All-time

Played	Won	Drawn	Lost	Points for	Points against
3	3	0	0	165	33

AUSTRIA
Final Tournaments:
Austria has not qualified to compete in any of the RWC Final Tournaments.

Qualifying Rounds:
Biggest win   3-0 v Yugoslavia 1997
Biggest defeat   6-36 v Ukraine 1997
All-time

Played	Won	Drawn	Lost	Points for	Points against
4	1	0	3	15	82

BAHAMAS
Final Tournaments:
Bahamas has not qualified to compete in any FWC Final Tournaments.

Qualifying Rounds:
Biggest win   37-23 v Barbados 1999
Biggest defeat   3-24 v Bermuda 1999
All-time

Played	Won	Drawn	Lost	Points for	Points against
2	1	0	1	40	47

BARBADOS
Final Tournaments:
Barbados has not qualified to compete in any Rugby World Cup Final Tournaments.

Qualifying Rounds:
Biggest win   None
Biggest defeat   3-52 v Bermuda 1999
All-time

Played	Won	Drawn	Lost	Points for	Points against
2	0	0	2	26	89

SECTION 2 – THE MODERN GAME

BELGIUM
Final Tournaments:
Belgium has not qualified to compete in any of the RWC Final Tournaments.

Qualifying Rounds:
Biggest win   42-3 v Switzerland 1995
Biggest defeat   13-83 v Romania 1997
All-time

Played	Won	Drawn	Lost	Points for	Points against
7	1	0	6	92	258

BERMUDA
Final Tournaments:
Bermuda has not qualified to compete in any of the RWC Final Tournaments.

Qualifying Rounds:
Biggest win   52-3 v Barbados 1997
Biggest defeat   8-68 v Chile 1997
All-time

Played	Won	Drawn	Lost	Points for	Points against
5	3	0	2	139	140

BOTSWANA
Final Tournaments:
Botswana has not qualified for any of the RWC Final Tournaments.

Qualifying Rounds:
Biggest win   None
Biggest defeat   13-53 v Gulf 1996
All-time

Played	Won	Drawn	Lost	Points for	Points against
2	0	0	2	26	73

BRAZIL
Final Tournaments
Brazil has not qualified to compete in any of the RWC Final Tournaments.

Qualifying Rounds
Biggest win   None
Biggest defeat 0-40 v Trinidad & Tobago 1996
All-time

Played	Won	Drawn	Lost	Points for	Points against
1	0	0	1	0	41

BULGARIA
Final Tournaments:
Bulgaria has not qualified to compete in any RWC Final Tournaments.

Qualifying Rounds:
Biggest win   None
Biggest defeat 0-89 v Latvia 1997
All-time

Played	Won	Drawn	Lost	Points for	Points against
4	0	0	4	44	171

CANADA
Final Tournaments:
Canada have played in three of the RWC Finals and qualified for them all.

Biggest win   37- 4 v Tonga 1987
Biggest defeat 19-46 v Ireland 1987
All-time

Played	Won	Drawn	Lost	Points for	Points against
10	4	0	6	168	-202

Qualifying Rounds:
Biggest win   38-15 v Uruguay 1999
Biggest defeat 28-54 v Argentina 1999

All-time

Played	Won	Drawn	Lost	Points for	Points against
7	5	0	2	164	121

SECTION 2 – THE MODERN GAME

CHILE
Final Tournaments:
Chile has not qualified to compete in any of the RWC Final Tournaments.

Qualifying Rounds:
Biggest win   68-8 v Bermuda 1997
Biggest defeat   7-70 v Argentina 1995
All-time

Played	Won	Drawn	Lost	Points for	Points against
7	3	0	4	205	149

COOK ISLANDS
Final Tournaments:
Cook Islands has not qualified for any of the RWC Final Tournaments.

Qualifying Rounds
Biggest win   40-0 v Tahiti 1997
Biggest defeat   12-68 v Tonga 1997
All-time

Played	Won	Drawn	Lost	Points for	Points against
4	2	0	2	81	140

IVORY COAST
Final Tournaments:
Only qualified for the RWC Finals in 1995.
Biggest win   None
Biggest defeat   0- 89 v Scotland 1995
All-time

Played	Won	Drawn	Lost	Points for	Points against
3	0	0	3	29	172

Qualifying Rounds:
Biggest win   17-10 v Zimbabwe 1995
Biggest defeat   0-32 v Zimbabwe 1999
All-time

Played	Won	Drawn	Lost	Points for	Points against
11	4	0	7	106	163

CROATIA
Final Tournaments:
Croatia has not taken part in any of the previous RWC Final Tournaments.

Qualifying Rounds:
Biggest win   60-5 v Moldova 1997
Biggest defeat   15-29 v Georgia 1997
All-time

Played	Won	Drawn	Lost	Points for	Points against
8	6	0	2	297	183

CZECH REPUBLIC
Final Tournaments:
Czech Republic has not qualified for any of the RWC Final Tournaments.

Qualifying Rounds:
Biggest win   34-7 v Sweden 1995 & 28-0 v Israel 1995
Biggest defeat   8-104 v Italy 1994
All-time

Played	Won	Drawn	Lost	Points for	Points against
11	4	0	7	201	312

DENMARK
Final Tournaments:
Denmark has not qualified to compete in any of the RWC Final Tournaments.

Qualifying Rounds:
Biggest win   26-12 v Switzerland 1991
Biggest defeat   3-102 v Italy 1997
All-time

Played	Won	Drawn	Lost	Points for	Points against
9	3	0	6	77	269

ENGLAND
Final Tournaments:
Have taken part in all the RWC Finals Tournaments.

SECTION 2 – THE MODERN GAME

Biggest win   60-7 v Japan 1987
Biggest defeat   29-45 v New Zealand 1995 (Semi-final)
All-time

Played	Won	Drawn	Lost	Points for	Points against
16	10	0	6	384	254

Qualifying Rounds:
Biggest win   110-0 Netherlands 1998
Biggest defeat   None
All-time

Played	Won	Drawn	Lost	Points for	Points against
2	2	0	0	133	15

FIJI
Final Tournaments:
Fiji Qualified in 1987 and 1999 RWC Finals, but not in any others.

Biggest win   28-9 v Argentina 1987
Biggest defeat   13-74 v New Zealand 1987
All-time

Played	Won	Drawn	Lost	Points for	Points against
7	1	0	6	99	195

Qualifying Rounds:
Biggest win   53-7 v Cook Islands 1999
Biggest defeat   20-66 v Australia 1999
All-time

Played	Won	Drawn	Lost	Points for	Points against
7	5	0	2	177	150

FRANCE
Final Tournaments:
France have played in all RWC Finals and have never had to qualify.

Biggest win   70-12 v Zimbabwe 1987
Biggest defeat   9-29 v New Zealand 1987 (The Final)

All-time

Played	Won	Drawn	Lost	Points for	Points against
16	12	1	3	491	244

Qualifying Rounds:
France has not needed to compete in any of the Rugby World Cup Qualifying Rounds.

GEORGIA
Final Tournaments:
Georgia has not qualified to compete in any of the previous RWC Final Tournaments.

Qualifying Rounds:
Biggest win   29-15 v Croatia 1999
Biggest defeat   0-70 v Ireland 1998
All-time

Played	Won	Drawn	Lost	Points for	Points against
10	4	0	6	146	259

GERMANY
Final Tournaments:
Germany has not qualified to compete in any of the RWC Final Tournaments.

Qualifying Rounds:
Biggest win   56-11 v Andorra 1997
Biggest defeat   5-67 v Russia 1995
All-time

Played	Won	Drawn	Lost	Points for	Points against
9	4	0	5	177	231

GUYANA
Guyana has withdrawn from the Rugby World Cup 1999 tournament.

SECTION 2 – THE MODERN GAME

HONG KONG
Final Tournaments:
Hong Kong has not qualified for any of the RWC Final Tournaments.

Qualifying Rounds:
Biggest win   164-13 v Singapore 1995 93 - 0 v Thailand 1995
Biggest defeat   19-39 South Korea 1988
All-time

Played	Won	Drawn	Lost	Points for	Points against
9	5	0	4	427	171

HUNGARY
Final Tournaments:
Hungary has not qualified for any of the RWC Final Tournaments.

Qualifying Rounds:
Biggest win   16-3 v Lithuania 1997
Biggest defeat   8-67 v Israel 1995
All-time

Played	Won	Drawn	Lost	Points for	Points against
5	2	0	3	58	146

IRELAND
Final Tournament:
Only had to qualify for 1999.

Biggest win   55-11 v Zimbabwe 1991
Biggest defeat   12-32 v France 1995
All-time

Played	Won	Drawn	Lost	Points for	Points against
12	6	0	6	324	274

Qualifying Rounds:
Biggest win   70-0 v Georgia 1998
Biggest defeat   None
All-time

Played	Won	Drawn	Lost	Points for	Points against
2	2	0	0	123	35

ISRAEL
Final Tournaments:
Israel has not qualified to compete in any of the RWC Final Tournaments.

Qualifying Rounds:
Biggest win   67-8 v Hungary 1995
Biggest defeat   0-56 v Netherlands 1995
All-time

Played	Won	Drawn	Lost	Points for	Points against
11	2	1	8	154	255

ITALY
Final Tournaments:
Have made all the RWC Finals.

Biggest win   30-9 v USA 1991
Biggest defeat   6-70 v New Zealand 1987
All-time

Played	Won	Drawn	Lost	Points for	Points against
9	3	0	6	166	280

Qualifying Rounds:
Biggest win   104-8 v Czech Republic 1995 &
                    102-3 v Denmark 1999
Biggest defeat   19-29 v Wales 1995
All-time

Played	Won	Drawn	Lost	Points for	Points against
13	11	0	2	595	182

JAPAN
Final Tournaments:
Japan weren't in the first RWC Final qualifiers, but qualified in 1991, 1995 and are one of the final 16 this year.

Biggest win   52-8 v Zimbabwe 1991
Biggest defeat   17-145 v New Zealand 1995

043

SECTION 2 – THE MODERN GAME

All-time

Played	Won	Drawn	Lost	Points for	Points against
9	1	0	8	177	462

Qualifying Rounds:
Biggest Win   134-6 v Chinese Taipei 1998
Biggest Defeat   11-37 v Western Samoa 1991
All-time

Played	Won	Drawn	Lost	Points for	Points against
14	12	0	2	753	169

KENYA
Final Tournaments:
Kenya has not qualified to compete in any of the RWC Final Tournaments.

Qualifying Rounds:
Biggest win   37-18 v Arabian Gulf 1997
Biggest defeat   9-60 v Namibia 1995
All-time

Played	Won	Drawn	Lost	Points for	Points against
5	2	0	3	82	195

LATVIA
Final Tournaments:
Latvia has not qualified to compete in any of the RWC Final Tournaments.

Qualifying Rounds:
Biggest win   89-0 v Bulgaria 1997
Biggest defeat   5-27 v Germany 1995
All-time

Played	Won	Drawn	Lost	Points for	Points against
6	4	0	2	177	85

LITHUANIA
Final Tournaments:
Lithuania has not qualified to compete in any of the RWC Final Tournaments.

Qualifying Rounds:
Biggest win   26-3 v Luxembourg 1996
Biggest defeat   17-84 v Sweden 1997
All-time

Played	Won	Drawn	Lost	Points for	Points against
6	1	0	5	81	195

LUXEMBOURG
Final Tournaments:
Luxembourg has not qualified to compete in any of the RWC Final Tournaments.

Qualifying Rounds:
Biggest win   None
Biggest defeat   3-26 v Lithuania 1996
All-time

Played	Won	Drawn	Lost	Points for	Points against
4	0	0	4	27	116

MALAYSIA
Final Tournaments:
Malaysia has not qualified to compete in any of the RWC Final Tournaments.

Qualifying Rounds:
Biggest win   23-18 v Sri Lanka 1995
Biggest defeat   0-102 v South Korea 1991 & 9-97 v Japan 1995
All-time

Played	Won	Drawn	Lost	Points for	Points against
8	1	0	7	81	390

MOLDOVA
Final Tournaments:
Moldova has not qualified to compete in any of the RWC Final Tournaments.

SECTION 2 – THE MODERN GAME

Qualifying Rounds:
Biggest win   31-7 v Norway 1997
Biggest defeat   5-60 v Croatia 1997
All-time

Played	Won	Drawn	Lost	Points for	Points against
4	2	0	2	53	81

MOROCCO
Final Tournaments:
Morocco has not qualified to compete in any of the RWC Final Tournaments.

Qualifying Rounds:
Biggest win   15-9 v Zimbabwe 1998
Biggest defeat   0-16 v Zimbabwe 1991
All-time

Played	Won	Drawn	Lost	Points for	Points against
13	5	1	6	127	167

NAMIBIA
Final Tournaments:
Namibia has not qualified to compete in any of the RWC Final Tournaments, although they will appear in the 1999 final stages.

Qualifying Rounds:
Biggest wins   64-20 v Arabian Gulf & 60 - 9 v Kenya 1995
Biggest defeat   17-20 v Tunisia 1999
All-time

Played	Won	Drawn	Lost	Points for	Points against
11	8	1	2	345	171

THE NETHERLANDS
Final Tournaments:
The Netherlands has not qualified to compete in any of the past RWC Final Tournaments.

Qualifying Rounds:
Biggest win   56-0 v Israel 1995
Biggest defeat   0-110 v England 1998
All-time

Played	Won	Drawn	Lost	Points for	Points against
19	11	0	8	427	550

NEW ZEALAND
Final Tournaments:
Have always gone straight through to the RWC Final Tournaments.

Biggest win   145-17 v Japan 1995
Biggest defeat   6-16 v Australia 1991
All-time

Played	Won	Drawn	Lost	Points for	Points against
18	16	0	2	768	245

NORWAY
Final Tournaments:
Norway has not qualified to compete in any of the RWC Final Tournaments.

Qualifying Rounds:
Biggest win   22-7 v Bulgaria 1997
Biggest defeat   6-44 v Latvia 1996
All-time

Played	Won	Drawn	Lost	Points for	Points against
4	1	0	3	42	125

PAPUA NEW GUINEA
Final Tournaments:
Papua New Guinea has not qualified to compete in any of the RWC Final Tournaments.

Qualifying Rounds:
Biggest win   92-6 v Tahiti 1997
Biggest defeat   19-22 v Cook Islands 1996

SECTION 2 – THE MODERN GAME

All-time
Played	Won	Drawn	Lost	Points for	Points against
2	1	0	1	111	28

PARAGUAY
Final Tournaments:
Paraguay has not qualified to compete in any of the past Rugby World Cup Final Tournaments.

Qualifying Rounds:
Biggest win   25-24 v Chile 1995
Biggest defeat   3-67 v Uruguay 1995
All-time
Played	Won	Drawn	Lost	Points for	Points against
5	1	0	4	40	239

POLAND
Final Tournaments:
Poland has not qualified to compete in any of the Rugby World Cup Final Tournaments.

Qualifying Rounds:
Biggest win   23-6 v Georgia 1995
Biggest defeat   7-49 v The Netherlands 1997
All-time
Played	Won	Drawn	Lost	Points for	Points against
6	2	0	4	86	138

PORTUGAL
Final Tournaments:
Portugal has not qualified to compete in any of the Rugby World Cup Final Tournaments.

Qualifying Rounds:
Biggest win   5-110 v Andorra 1995
Biggest defeat   11-102 v Wales 1995

All-time

Played	Won	Drawn	Lost	Points for	Points against
15	6	0	9	284	467

ROMANIA
Final Tournaments:
Romania were invited to the first RWC Final Tournament, but haven't qualified or appeared until 1999/

Biggest win   21-20 v Zimbabwe 1987 & 12-55 v France 1987
Biggest defeat   28-55 v Scotland 1987
All-time

Played	Won	Drawn	Lost	Points for	Points against
9	1	0	8	106	264

Qualifying Rounds:
Biggest win   83-13 v Belgium 1999
Biggest defeat   35-53 v Ireland 1998
All-time

Played	Won	Drawn	Lost	Points for	Points against
13	9	0	4	490	210

RUSSIA
Final Tournaments:
Russia has not qualified to compete in any of the past RWC Final Tournaments.

Qualifying Rounds:
Biggest win   67-5 v Germany 1995
Biggest defeat   0-30 v Romania 1995
All-time

Played	Won	Drawn	Lost	Points for	Points against
8	4	0	4	208	141

SCOTLAND
Final Tournaments:
Played in the first three RWC Final Tournaments and only had to qualify for the 1999 games.

SECTION 2 – THE MODERN GAME

Biggest win   89-0 v Cote d'Ivoire 1995
Biggest defeat   30-48 v New Zealand 1995
All-time

Played	Won	Drawn	Lost	Points for	Points against
14	8	1	5	479	338

Qualifying Rounds:
Biggest win   85-3 v Spain 1998
Biggest defeat   None
All-time

Played	Won	Drawn	Lost	Points for	Points against
2	2	0	0	170	14

SINGAPORE
Final Tournaments:
Singapore has not qualified to compete in any of the RWC Final Tournaments.

Qualifying Rounds:
Biggest win   None
Biggest defeat   13-164 v Hong Kong 1995
All-time

Played	Won	Drawn	Lost	Points for	Points against
8	0	0	8	55	542

SOUTH AFRICA
Final Tournaments:
South Africa did not compete in 1987 or 1991 due to apartheid.
Biggest win   42-14 v Western Samoa 1995
Biggest defeat   None
All-time

Played	Won	Drawn	Lost	Points for	Points against
6	6	0	0	144	67

Qualifying Rounds:
South Africa, as the Host Nation, didn't need to compete in the 1995 Qualifying Rounds.

SOUTH KOREA
Final Tournaments:
South Korea has not qualified to compete in any of the RWC Final Tournaments.

Qualifying Rounds:
Biggest win   102-0 v Malaysia 1991 & 90-3 v Singapore 1995
Biggest defeat 7-74 v Western Samoa 1991
All-time

Played	Won	Drawn	Lost	Points for	Points against
18	8	0	9	712	506

SPAIN
Final Tournaments:
Spain has not qualified to compete in any of the past RWC Final Tournaments.

Qualifying Rounds:
Biggest win   67-3 v Belgium 1995 & 62-3 v Andorra 1999
Biggest defeat 3-85 v Scotland 1999
All-time

Played	Won	Drawn	Lost	Points for	Points against
14	10	0	4	395	296

SRI LANKA
Final Tournaments
Sri Lanka has not qualified to compete in any of the Rugby World Cup Final Tournaments.

Qualifying Rounds:
Biggest win   37-15 v Malaysia 1997
Biggest defeats 6-68 v South Korea 1991 & 3-67 v Japan 1995
All-time

Played	Won	Drawn	Lost	Points for	Points against
10	4	0	6	165	283

SECTION 2 – THE MODERN GAME

SWEDEN
Final Tournaments:
Sweden has not qualified to compete in any of the RWC Final Tournaments.

Qualifying Rounds:
Biggest win   84-17 v Lithuania 1997
Biggest defeat   7-34 v Czech Republic 1995
All-time

Played	Won	Drawn	Lost	Points for	Points against
11	7	0	4	331	184

SWITZERLAND
Final Tournaments:
Switzerland has not qualified to compete in any of the RWC Final Tournaments.

Qualifying Rounds:
Biggest win   31-3 v Austria 1997
Biggest defeat   0-40 v Spain 1995 & 3-42 v Belgium 1995
All-time

Played	Won	Drawn	Lost	Points for	Points against
12	3	1	8	109	246

TAHITI
Final Tournaments:
Tahiti has not qualified to compete in any of the Rugby World Cup Final Tournaments.

Qualifying Rounds:
Biggest win   None
Biggest defeat   6-92 v Papua New Guinea 1997
All-time

Played	Won	Drawn	Lost	Points for	Points against
2	0	0	2	6	132

TAIWAN
Final Tournaments:
Taiwan (Chinese Taipei) has not qualified to compete in any of the past RWC Final Tournaments.

Qualifying Rounds:
Biggest win   86-3 v Singapore 1991
Biggest defeat   6-134 v Japan 1999
All-time

Played	Won	Drawn	Lost	Points for	Points against
11	7	0	4	342	381

THAILAND
Final Tournaments:
Thailand has not qualified to compete in any of the RWC Final Tournaments.

Qualifying Rounds:
Biggest win   69-5 v Singapore 1991
Biggest defeat   7-108 v Japan 1995
All-time

Played	Won	Drawn	Lost	Points for	Points against
8	3	0	5	146	347

TONGA
Final Tournaments:
Tonga only appeared in the 1995 RWC Finals Tournaments, although they did try to qualify for 1999.

Biggest win   29-11 v Cote d'Ivoire 1995
Biggest defeat   5-41 v Scotland 1995
All-time

Played	Won	Drawn	Lost	Points for	Points against
6	1	0	5	73	188

Qualifying Rounds:
Biggest win   82-15 v Korea 1999
Biggest defeat   0-74 v Australia 1999

SECTION 2 – THE MODERN GAME

All-time
Played	Won	Drawn	Lost	Points for	Points against
14	6	0	8	415	329

TRINIDAD & TOBAGO
Final Tournaments:
Trinidad & Tobago has not qualified to compete in any of the Rugby World Cup Final Tournaments.

Qualifying Rounds:
Biggest win   40-0 v Brazil 1996
Biggest defeat   6-52 v Bermuda 1997
All-time
Played	Won	Drawn	Lost	Points for	Points against
3	1	0	2	52	87

TUNISIA
Final Tournaments:
Tunisia has not qualified to compete in any of the past RWC Final Tournaments.

Qualifying Rounds:
Biggest win   52-5 v Kenya 1997
Biggest defeat   13-24 v Zimbabwe 1995
All-time
Played	Won	Drawn	Lost	Points for	Points against
9	4	0	5	154	145

UKRAINE
Final Tournaments:
Ukraine has not qualified to compete in any of the RWC Final Tournaments.

Qualifying Rounds:
Biggest win   60-0 v Yugoslavia 1996
Biggest defeat   17-39 v Romania 1998

All-time
Played	Won	Drawn	Lost	Points for	Points against
8	6	0	2	274	108

URUGUAY
Final Tournaments:
Uruguay has not qualified to compete in any of the past Rugby World Cup Final Tournaments. Uruguay have advanced to Round D of the Americas Tournament to be played in August.

Qualifying Rounds:
Biggest win   67-3 v Paraguay 1995
Biggest defeat   0-55 v Argentina 1999
All-time
Played	Won	Drawn	Lost	Points for	Points against
12	7	0	5	280	256

USA
Final Tournaments:
The USA were invited to the first RWC Final, but had to qualify for 1995 and 1999.

Biggest win   21-18 v Japan 1987
Biggest defeat   12-47 v Australia 1987
All-time
Played	Won	Drawn	Lost	Points for	Points against
6	1	0	5	63	212

Qualifying Rounds:
Biggest win   60-3 v Bermuda 1995
Biggest defeat   24-52 v Argentina 1999
All-time
Played	Won	Drawn	Lost	Points for	Points against
10	3	0	7	181	215

SECTION 2 – THE MODERN GAME

WALES
Final Tournaments:
Wales were invited to take part in the first three RWC Finals, but had to compete for 1999.

Biggest win   57-10 v Japan 1995
Biggest defeat   6-49 v New Zealand 1987
All-time

Played	Won	Drawn	Lost	Points for	Points against
12	7	0	5	244	236

Qualifying Rounds:
Biggest win   102 - 11 v Portugal 1995
Biggest defeat   None
All-time

Played	Won	Drawn	Lost	Points for	Points against
4	4	0	0	201	39

WESTERN SAMOA
Final Tournaments:
Took part in 1995 for the first time and qualified for the 1999 RWC Finals Tournaments.

Biggest win   42-18 v Italy 1995
Biggest defeat   14-42 v South Africa 1995
All-time

Played	Won	Drawn	Lost	Points for	Points against
8	4	0	4	170	192

Qualifying Rounds:
Biggest win   74-7 v South Korea 1991
Biggest defeat   13-25 v Australia 1999
All-time

Played	Won	Drawn	Lost	Points for	Points against
6	4	0	2	182	92

YUGOSLAVIA
Final Tournaments:
Yugoslavia has not qualified to compete in any of the RWC Final Tournaments.

Qualifying Rounds:
Biggest win　　　　8-0 v Switzerland 1997
Biggest defeat　　　0-60 v Ukraine 1996
All-time

Played	Won	Drawn	Lost	Points for	Points against
5	2	0	3	24	96

ZAMBIA
Final Tournaments:
Zambia has not qualified to compete in any of the RWC Final Tournaments.

Qualifying Rounds:
Biggest win　　　　20-13 v Botswana 1997
Biggest defeat　　　30-44 v Arabian Gulf 1997
All-time

Played	Won	Drawn	Lost	Points for	Points against
2	1	0	1	50	57

ZIMBABWE
Final Tournaments:
Zimbabwe played in the first RWC qualifiers, but lost all their matches.
Biggest win　　　　None
Biggest defeat　　　12 - 70 v France 1987
All-time

Played	Won	Drawn	Lost	Points for	Points against
6	0	0	6	84	309

Qualifying Rounds:
Biggest win　　　　43-9 v Tunisia 1999
Biggest defeat　　　14-39 v Namibia 1999
All-time

Played	Won	Drawn	Lost	Points for	Points against
14	8	0	6	345	237

SECTION 2 – THE MODERN GAME

World Rugby Rankings May 1999

(Complied from international matches played through 1 May 1999)

Rank	Team	Previous ranking	Change
1	South Africa	(1)	
2	Australia	(2)	
3	New Zealand	(3)	
4	England	(4)	
5	Scotland	(8)	+3
6	France	(5)	-1
8	Samoa	(7)	-1
9	Ireland	(9)	
10	Wales	(10)	
11	Italy	(11)	
12	Argentina	(12)	
13	Canada	(13)	
14	Tonga	(14)	
15	Hong Kong	(15)	
16	United States	(16)	
17	Japan	(17)	
18	Romania	(18)	
19	Uruguay	(19)	
20	Chile	(20)	
21	Namibia	(21)	
22	South Korea	(25)	+3
23	Spain	(22)	-1
24	Portugal	(23)	-1
25	Netherlands	(24)	-1
26	Morocco	(26)	
27	Georgia	(27)	
28	Zimbabwe	(28)	
29	Croatia	(29)	
30	Ivory Coast	(30)	
31	Russia	(31)	
32	Tunisia	(32)	
33	Ukraine	(33)	
34	Paraguay	(34)	
35	Poland	(35)	

Rank	Team	Previous ranking	Change
36	Belgium	(36)	
37	Germany	(37)	
38	Czech Republic	(38)	
39	Taiwan	(N/A)	
40	Denmark	(39)	-1
41	Sri Lanka	(N/A)	

New results contributing to the above rankings

1997

November 03	South Korea 60	Sri Lanka 20
November 05	Hong Kong 66	Sri Lanka 13
November 06	Japan 101	Taiwan 12
November 09	Hong Kong 114	Taiwan 12

1998

January 17	Taiwan 31	Sri Lanka 27
October 24	Taiwan 30	Hong Kong 12
October 27	Japan 134	Taiwan 6
October 31	South Korea 81	Taiwan 21
November 12	Hong Kong 45	Sri Lanka 3
December 10	South Korea 90	Sri Lanka 3
December 12	Japan 64	Taiwan 11
December 16	Japan 116	Sri Lanka 0
December 16	South Korea 69	Taiwan 5
December 18	Taiwan 38	Sri Lanka 20

1999

April 03	Uruguay 33	Portugal 24
April 04	South Korea 7	8Netherlands 14
April 10	Scotland 36	France 22
April 10	Ireland 39	Italy 30
April 11	Wales 32	England 31
April 17	Tonga 58	South Korea 26
April 18	Uruguay 18	Morocco 3

SECTION 2 – THE MODERN GAME

IRB Fourth General Meeting in Buenos Aires
April 15, 1999

Over a hundred of the world's most senior rugby administrators attended the International Rugby Board's Fourth General Meeting in Buenos Aires, Argentina. Vernon Pugh QC, the IRB Executive Council Chairman, said membership of national unions and associations had grown from seventy to eighty-four since the third General Meeting, held in Rome in October 1996.

In the week-long meeting, applications to join the IRB were considered from Cameroon, Columbia, India and Niue Island, in the South Pacific. On the continuing drive to secure a place for rugby in the Olympics, Pugh said the game fulfiled all the criteria for participation status, "However, the Games are already fully stretched numerically following the inclusion in recent years of 'minor' sports. We are very happy to put forward fifteen-a-side rather than sevens, the preference expressed at the Rome General Meeting. We do not wish to be criticised for providing a second-best version."

Pugh told delegates the time had come for individual unions to work towards entry to the Olympics. "We have prepared an Olympic package and will be asking all unions to work on our behalf with their own National Olympic Associations. We recognise the development of good personal contacts, political influence and persistence are fundamental requirements," he said.

The decisions at the Council's Annual Meeting were numerous and important in the continuing advancement of Rugby Union as a world sport. The membership was increased by five to eighty-nine Unions and Regional Associations with the admission of Cameroon, Columbia, India, Peru and the South Pacific Island of Niue.

Vernon Pugh QC said that the IRB's regionalisation strategy was continuing to gain momentum and support throughout the world. "We have made considerable progress in developing regional organisations for Europe, where FIRA is already well-established, Africa (CAR), South America (CONSUR) and Asia (ARFU) to enable us to deliver coaching, refereeing and other game development programmes in a systematic and organised manner," he commented.

Plans are being developed to set up regional competitions where they do not presently exist and in early June fourteen Pacific unions came together at a meeting with senior Council officials during the South Pacific

Games, in Guam. The intention according to Pugh was to work towards the formation of a new Oceania Regional Association.

Committee chairman Bernard Lapasset, of France, said Council has agreed a set of criteria to be applied to the formulation of a schedule of international matches, tours and tournaments for the period 2000-2005. Lapasset then announced, "Very detailed discussions were involved and the schedule has now been completed in accordance with the criteria. It will be circulated to the unions involved before being made public."

He said a special feature of the schedule is the inclusion for the first time of Argentina, Canada, Fiji, Italy, Japan, Romania, Samoa, Tonga and USA. "This will provide these unions with set fixtures against the senior national teams or, by arrangement, the 'A' teams of the major unions. We intend to develop similar schedules for sevens, women's and age grade rugby."

"The development of the criteria and schedule has been a difficult and time-consuming exercise requiring compromise on the part of all unions as they meet their responsibilities for promoting the game worldwide," Lapasset added.

The IRB Council has agreed to the establishment of an annual international World Sevens Series, to be implemented as soon as reasonably practical. "It is hoped the new series can kick off in December of this year. However there is much still to do in terms of completing commercial arrangements with the brokers and confirming the selected venues," Lapasset explained.

The 1999 Conference on the Playing of the Game will take place in Sydney, Australia in early December. Those attending will include leading coaches, players and referees along with National Directors of Rugby.

SECTION 3 – THE FIVES NATIONS CHAMPIONSHIP

The Five Nations Championship

The first Five Nations Championship was competed for between England, Ireland, Wales and Scotland in 1882/83, with England winning the title. The current Five Nation Champions are Scotland who took the title on Points difference from England.

Between the years 1915-19 and 1940-46 there were no matches due to the world wars. In addition, the championships of 1883, 1885, 1888, 1889, 1897, 1888 and 1914 were not completed for various reasons. While in 1972 the championship was not completed when Scotland and Wales both refused to travel to Ireland because of internal security issues.

Until 1993 the championship could be shared but from 1994 points difference was used to find just the one overall winner. Below are the all-time records of the five competing nations and an expanded look at the 1999 Championship. A 'Grand Slam' occurs when the winning nation completes a full round of wins within one single championship. A Triple Crown occurs when one nation wins three out of the four games to take the championship.

ENGLAND
1883, 1884, 1886*, 1890*, 1892, 1910, 1912*, 1913, 1914, 1920*, 1921, 1923, 1924, 1928, 1930, 1932*, 1934, 1937, 1939*, 1947*, 1953, 1954*, 1957, 1958, 1960*, 1963*, 1973**, 1980, 1991, 1992, 1995, 1996

Summary
32 wins (10 shared), 20 Triple Crowns (5 of which were in seasons France did not play, 11 were also Grand Slams
Grand Slams: 1913, 1914, 1921, 1923, 1924, 1928, 1957, 1980, 1991, 1992, 1995
Triple Crowns: 1883, 1884, 1892, 1934, 1937, 1954, 1960, 1996, 1997

FRANCE
1954*, 1955*, 1959, 1960*, 1961, 1962, 1967, 1968, 1970*, 1973**, 1977, 1981, 1983*, 1986*, 187, 1988*, 1989, 1993, 1997, 1998

Summary
19 wins (8 Shared), five Grand Slams 1968, 1977, 1981, 1987, 1997
IRELAND
1894, 1896, 1899, 1906*, 1912*, 1926*,1927*, 1932*, 1935, 1939*, 1948, 1949, 1951, 1973**, 1974, 1982, 1983*, 1985
Summary
18 wins (8 shared), One Grand Slam in 1948, Triple Crowns in 1894, 1899, 1949, 1982, 1985

SCOTLAND
1886*, 1887, 1890*, 1891, 1895, 1901, 1903, 1904, 1907, 1920*, 1925, 1926*, 1927*, 1929, 1933, 1938, 1964*, 1973**, 1984, 1986*, 1990, 1999
Summary
21 wins (8 shared), including 10 Triple Crowns (7 in seasons that France did not play)
Grand Slams: 1925, 1984, 1990
Triple Crowns: 1891, 1895, 1901, 1903, 1907, 1933, 1938

WALES
1893, 1900, 1902, 1905, 1906*, 1908, 1909, 1911, 1920*, 1922, 1931, 1932*, 1936, 1939, 1947, 1950, 1952, 1954*, 1955*, 1956, 1964*, 1965, 1966, 1969, 1970*, 1971, 1973**, 1975, 1976, 1978, 1979, 1988*, 1994
Summary
33 wins (11 shared), seventeen Triple Crowns (six in years that France did not play), six of which were also Grand Slams.
Grand Slams: 1911, 1950, 1952, 1971, 1976, 1978
Triple Crowns: 1893, 1900, 1902, 1905, 1908, 1909, 1965, 1969, 1977, 1979, 1988

* Indicates a shared title
** indicates a five-way tie for the championship

SECTION 3 – THE FIVES NATIONS CHAMPIONSHIP

Lloyds TSB Five Nations Round-Up 1999

	P	W	D	L	F	A	PTS
Scotland	4	3	0	1	120	79	6
England	4	3	0	1	103	78	6
Wales	4	2	0	2	109	12	6
Ireland	4	1	0	3	66	90	2
France	4	1	0	3	75	100	2

Five Nations 1999 Match-By-Match Summary

Sunday 11 April – Wales 32-31 England
Centre Scott Gibbs shattered England's Grand Slam dreams with an injury time try that gave Wales a 32-31 victory in a dramatic Five Nations finale. The dazzling solo effort followed by Neil Jenkins' conversion meant that Scotland landed the championship for the first time since 1990. England always had the upper hand after first half tries from Richard Hill, Dan Luger and Steve Hanley, but Welsh hearts were strong and Neil Jenkins was superb with eight successful kicks.

Saturday 10 April – France 22-36 Scotland
Scotland kept their Five Nations title hopes alive by recording their highest points score against France in eighty-nine years in an amazing match in Paris. After France scored in the opening moments of the game, Scotland, led by an inspired Glenn Metcalfe, went on the rampage and scythed through the French defence with five tries in twenty minutes to race into a 33-12 lead before being pegged back to 33-22 at the break. The only score in a quieter second half came from a Kenny Logan penalty.

Saturday 20 March – England 21-10 France
A brilliant display of penalty kicking from teenager Jonny Wilkinson inspired England to a vital Five Nations win over France at Twickenham. The victory, which keeps England's Grand Slam ambitions on track, was made possible by a display of accuracy from the Newcastle centre.

Saturday 20 March – Scotland 30-13 Ireland
Scotland continued their domination over the Irish with an impressive 30-13 Five Nations victory at Murrayfield. Scotland ran in four superb

tries in a stunning display of running rugby to keep alive their slender Five Nations Championship dreams. Star performer Gregor Townsend took centre stage and was at the centre of an inspirational display from the home backs, scoring one try, playing a major part in two others and dancing through the Irish defence as Scotland earned their eighth successive home win over their Gaelic rivals.

Saturday 6 March – France 33-34 Wales
In one of the truly great Five Nations games in recent years, Neil Jenkins kicked 19 points and Wales grabbed three sensational tries to edge out the French at Stade de France. Full credit to the Welsh who took on the French at their own running game and raced into a 28-18 half-time lead. The hosts came storming back, and fullback Emile Ntamack scored a hat-trick of tries but the Welsh clung on for a famous victory.

Saturday 6 March – Ireland 15-27 England
An inspirational display from captain Lawrence Dallaglio ensured England made it two wins out of two as the Irish saw their dreams of victory come to nought. Irish hopes were high after the fine performance against France, but England with Jonny Wilkinson kicking coolly, and their forwards back in dominating mode, left the home team living off the boot of stand-off David Humphreys. England, for whom Matt Perry and Tim Rodber scored tries, are now looking at Grand Slam and Triple Crown glory.

Saturday 22nd February – England 24-21 Scotland
England opened up their Five Nations account with a thrilling victory over Scotland to retain the Calcutta Cup at Twickenham. Scotland have not won at Twickenham since 1983 and it has been ten years since they last won the Calcutta Cup, but they gave England a real fight providing a great spectacle for rugby in the process.

Saturday 22nd February – Wales 23-29 Ireland
Fly-half David Humphreys made amends for missing a late penalty against France two weeks ago kicking 19 points to inspire Ireland to victory over Wales at Wembley. Humphreys, who missed a kick in injury time for Ireland when they went down 10-9 to the French, redeemed himself with two second half drop goals that proved the difference between the two sides. Humphreys also created the only try of the first half for Kevin Maggs.

SECTION 3 – THE FIVES NATIONS CHAMPIONSHIP

Saturday 6th February – Scotland 33-20 Wales
The Scots confounded the pre-match predictions, staging a late rally to win a thrilling six-try encounter. They started sensationally, John Leslie scoring after just twelve seconds although they went off the boil and with ten minutes remaining the scores were level at 20-20. Two late tries and the boot of Logan swept the home side to victory.

Saturday 6th February – Ireland 9-10 France
A below-par French side won a game in which they had led for only three minutes. Leading 9-0 and in control going into the final quarter, the visitors pulled back with a try for Dourthe and took the lead in the dying seconds with a CastaignËde penalty. Humphries, who missed four from seven kicks, could have won the game deep in injury time but he screwed his penalty just wide.

Five Nation Facts

- The tournament became the Five Nations when France first joined in 1910.

- The record for most points in a Five Nations match by a single player is 24 and three players share the spoils – Sebastian Viars: France (France v Ireland, 92); Rob Andrew: England (England v Scotland, 95); Christophe Lamaison (France v Scotland 97).

- The record for most points scored in a match by a nation is 60 by England V Wales in 1998.

- France established the biggest winning margin by beating Wales 51-0 in 1998. Wales however, did score 49 against France in 1910, a score that would be worth 69 with today's points system.

- Between 1932 and 1939 it once again reverted to a Four Nations Championship when the Home Unions banned France because of players being paid at club level.

- In 1888 and 1889 it was a Three Nations Tournament, England not competing as they refused to become a member of the newly formed International Rugby Board.

- The Tournaments of 1885, 1897 and 1898 were not completed because of variety of disputes between different countries. In 1972 event when Scotland and Wales chose not to play in Dublin because of violence in Ulster.

- Uniquely, the 1973 Championship was a five-way tie, with all countries winning two and losing two games.

- A Trophy was awarded in 1993, the following year Wales won the title on points difference – the first time such a tie break had been employed following its introduction the previous year. Until 1992 teams that were level on points shared the title.

- JPR Williams has been on the winning side the most with thirty-four wins in forty-four matches. Mike Gibson has been on the losing side the most with 28 in fifty-six matches. Willie – John McBride is the only one to have shared in seven drawn matches.

- England's WJA Davies had a remarkable success rate, never ending up on the losing side in twenty-one Five Nations games. His only 'blemish' being an 11-11 draw with France at Twickenham in 1922.

- Only two players have won all eight games they have played in – Charles Wade of England (1883-86) and Eric Bonneval of France (1985-88).

- Three players have lost all matches that they have participated in – JRW Morrow of Ireland (1883-88), Jacques Dedet of France (1910-13) and John Henderson of Scotland (1953-54).

- The record number of tries ever scored was in 1887 by George Lindsay's five in the match between Scotland and Wales.

- The clash between Wales and France in 1910 saw the highest number of conversions by Jack Bancroft when he made eight.

- The record for the most penalty goals in a match is seven; this is shared between Simon Hodgkinsoon in the England v Wales match in 1991 and the England v Scotland clash of 1995.

- Jean-Patrick Lecscarboura scored three drop goals in the France v

SECTION 3 – THE FIVES NATIONS CHAMPIONSHIP

England match of 1985. This is the highest recorded number for an individual in a match.

- Gavin Hastings leads the table for the points in his illustrious five nations career which lasted from 1986 until 1995. During this time he appeared thirty-six times, made four tries, 20 conversions, 77 penalty goals and scored 288 points. He didn't score one drop goal during this time.

- Jonathan Webb holds the Five Nations record for the most points in a season with 67 for England in 1992.

- In the Five Nations Championship Colin Deans holds the record for the most appearances in the starting line-up, having played thirty-seven times.

- Far and away the highest ever number of tries in a Five Nations career was made by Ian S Smith of Scotland. He played during 1924-1933 making thirty-one appearances and gaining 24 tries for his country.

- The oldest player ever to make a Five Nations appearance was Tommy Vile of Wales in 1921. He took to the field at the age of 38 years and 152 days.

- The youngest player ever to play in a Five Nations match is Frank Hewitt who, at the age of 17 years and 157 days, played for Ireland in the 1924 tournament.

- The Tallest players ever to grace the Five Nations competition are Matrin Batfield of England and Derwyn Jones of Wales. Both players are six foot ten inches, and appeared for their countries in the Nineties.

- No Scotsman has yet played forty-five Five Nations Games in his career, whereas a Frenchman, Welshman, Englishman and Irishman all have.

- The 1997 match between France and Scotland produced the highest number of points ever seen in a Five Nations game. Scotland gained 20 whereas, France prospered with a massive 47.

- Andy Irvine played for Scotland from 1973-83. This Scotsman, who played thirty-nine Five Nation games and scored 201 points. This is the second highest number of points a Scotsman has racked up, Gavin Hastings leads the table amongst all the member nations.

- In a dispute between the governing body of English Rugby Union – the RFU – and the other British home nations, England were expelled from the Five Nations championship of 1999, but were later reinstated. The Five Nations committee took the decision to expel England because they were not satisfied with the stance the RFU had taken. Italy were lined up as England's possible replacements. The dispute had centred on the division of money the RFU received in a deal from a satellite television company. In 1996 the RFU negotiated their own deal with Sky television. After threats of expulsion from the Five Nations tournament, the RFU agreed to give the other nations a share of the money, but in 1998 it emerged that the RFU had not to date, paid out any monies.

- Tommy Voyce of England and Jock Wemyss of Scotland, who scrummaged against each other at Twickenham in 1920, had only one eye each. Ironically, Voyce was also the blind-side flanker!

- Four Neilson brothers played for Scotland between the years of 1891 and 1900 in the Five Nations. The brothers were Walter, William, George and Robert.

- When Scotland played France in 1994, brothers Scott and Gavin Hastings both picked up their fiftieth international caps.

SECTION 4 – ALLIED DUNBAR PREMIERSHIP

Allied Dunbar Premiership

About The Allied Dunbar Competition

- The Allied Dunbar Premiership rugby competition began in the 1997/8 season with twenty-four clubs.

- The Allied Dunbar Premiership comprises divisions one and two from the old league, renamed Allied Dunbar One and Allied Dunbar Two.

- As part of the Mayfair Agreement, four new teams have joined Allied Dunbar Two from Jewsons National League Division One for 1998/9 – Leeds Tykes, London Welsh, Rugby and Worcester. Two clubs were additionally promoted to Allied Dunbar Premiership One, with play-offs taking place with the top two from AD2 and bottom 2 from AD1 to make up AD1 this season.

- There are now fourteen clubs in Allied Dunbar One and 14 in Allied Dunbar Two.

- Each of the fourteen clubs in each Premiership will play one another twice – home and away.

- There are two divisional winners – Allied Dunbar One (Newcastle Falcons in 97/8) and Allied Dunbar Two (Bedford Rugby in 97/98).

- A total of six hundred and seventy-six matches plus play-offs were played between September and May.

- Allied Dunbar made a sponsorship commitment for an initial three years (up to the end of the 1999/2000 season).

- The Allied Dunbar Premiership represents Allied Dunbar's first major sponsorship activity.

Allied Dunbar Premiership 1 Final Table 1998/99

Club	P	W	D	L	F	A	Points
Leicester	26	22	0	4	771	423	44
Northampton	26	19	0	7	754	556	38
Saracens	26	16	1	9	748	583	33
Harlequins	26	16	1	9	690	653	33
Wasps	26	15	1	10	717	506	31
Bath	26	15	0	11	698	574	30
London Irish	26	15	0	11	703	607	30
Newcastle	26	14	0	12	719	639	28
Richmond	26	11	2	13	720	715	22 *
Gloucester	26	9	1	16	554	643	19
Manchester Sale	26	9	1	16	604	731	19
London Scottish	26	8	0	18	491	734	16
Bedford	26	6	0	20	541	840	12
West Hartlepool	26	3	1	22	501	1007	7

* Deducted two points for postponing a league game

Allied Dunbar Premiership 2 Final Table 1998/99

Club	P	W	D	L	F	A	Points
Bristol	26	22	0	4	848	418	44
Rotherham	26	22	0	4	756	336	44
Worcester	26	18	0	8	716	409	34 *
London Welsh	26	17	0	9	662	552	34
Exeter	26	14	1	11	591	598	29
Leeds	26	16	0	10	713	367	28 **
Coventry	26	14	0	12	652	560	28
Orrell	26	12	0	14	566	483	24
Waterloo	26	12	0	14	419	634	24
Moseley	26	10	0	16	498	633	20
Rugby	26	9	0	17	425	660	18
Wakefield	26	6	0	20	469	812	12
Blackheath	26	5	0	21	419	842	10
Fylde	26	4	1	21	375	805	9

* Deducted two points for fielding an unregistered player
** Deducted four points for fielding an unregistered player

SECTION 4 – ALLIED DUNBAR PREMIERSHIP

- The Allied Dunbar Premiership clubs are governed by English Rugby Partnership – a private limited company owned 50% RFU; 33.33% English First Division Rugby and 16.66% by English Second Division.

- Allied Dunbar also sponsors the referees and match officials at all Allied Dunbar Premiership matches.

1998/99 Allied Dunbar Premiership Player Of The Season

The nominations and winners were as follows:

Allied Dunbar Premiership Player of the Season
Winner: Martin Johnson (Leicester Tigers)
Nominees: Scott Murray (Bedford), Va'aiga Tuigamala (Newcastle Falcons)

Allied Dunbar Premiership Young Player of the Season
Winner: Jonny Wilkinson (Newcastle Falcons)
Nominees: Iain Balshaw (Bath), Steve Hanley (Manchester Sale)

Allied Dunbar Premiership International Player of the Season
Winner: Scott Murray (Bedford)
Nominees: Keith Wood (NEC Harlequins), Shane Howarth (Manchester Sale)

Allied Dunbar Premiership Coach of the Season
Winner: Ian McGeechan (Northampton Saints)
Nominees: Dick Best (London Irish), John Wells (Leicester Tigers)

Allied Dunbar Premiership Fair Play Award
Winner: Wakefield

Allied Dunbar Premiership Unsung Hero of the Season
Winner: Chris McCarthy (NEC Harlequins)
Nominees: Alan Blease (Manchester Sale), Nathan Carter (Gloucester), Robbie Dickson (Manchester Sale), Ray Grieve (Newcastle Falcons), Derek Limmage (Leicester Tigers), Kieron McCarthy (London Irish), Roy Saunders (Worcester), Don Shaw (Blackheath), Mrs Jackie Thomas (Moseley)

Allied Dunbar Premiership Two Players' Player of the Season
Winner: John Dudley (Rotherham)
Nominees: Andy Currier (London Welsh), Paul Spence (Rotherham)

Allied Dunbar Premiership One Players' Player of the Season
Winner: Conor O'Shea (London Irish)
Nominees: Gary Armstrong (Newcastle Falcons), Neil Back (Leicester)

SECTION 4 – ALLIED DUNBAR PREMIERSHIP

Team-By-Team Run Down Of The Allied Dunbar Leagues And History Of The Teams

Bath FC
Ground
Recreation Ground
Bath
BA2 6PW
Stadium Capacity: 8,200
Colours:
Shirts: Blue, Black & White hoops with Adidas white stripes on sleeves
Shorts: Royal Blue
Change Shirts: Blue, Black, Amber and White hoops with Adidas white stripes on sleeves
Shorts :Royal Blue
History
Founded: 1865
Number of International Players: 55
Total number of individual caps: 817
First capped player: Frank 'Buster' Soane, England v Scotland at Leeds, 4 March 1893.
Most capped player:(72) Ieuan Evans for Wales.
Most tries in tests:(34) Ieuan Evans (33 for Wales, 1 for British Lions).
Most points in tests: 194 in 17 by Jon Webb (1990-93). Webb also scored 102 points in 16 tests as a Bristol player.

Prominent Players
Adedayo Adebayo

Position: Wing
Date of Birth: 30 November 1970
Place of Birth: Ibadan, Nigeria
Height: 5' 9"
Weight: 14st 7lbs

Educated at Kelly College, Devon, and Swansea University. Broke a number of England Schools under-15 and under-18 try scoring records. Joined Bath in 1989-90 while still a teenager, has played for the South West Division, England B and England A. Played just forty-four minutes of rugby in 1991-92 season, against Cork Constitution on 28 September, then suffered a serious knee injury which kept him out for the remainder of the season until September 1992. His career has been dogged by injury but he is now fully recovered to take up his place on the wing, where he is deceptively fast. A member of England's world-beating Sevens team at Edinburgh in 1993. Picked for England to tour Canada, playing in the Second Test. He was in the England squad for South Africa, summer 1994 but didn't win his first England cap until 1996 versus Italy. He then represented England on the tour of Argentina in 1997. He was Bath's top try-scorer in 1996/97 with 24 tries and was selected for the England squad for Australia 1997.

SECTION 4 – ALLIED DUNBAR PREMIERSHIP

Jon Callard
Position: Fullback
Date of Birth: 01 January 1966
Place of Birth: Leicester
Height: 5' 11"
Weight: 12st 10lbs

Educated at Bassaleg School, Newport, and St Paul's and St Mary's College, Cheltenham, formerly employed as a schoolmaster (PE) at Downside Abbey. Made his Newport debut as an eighteen-year-old against Bath and moved to the Recreation Ground near the end of the 1988-89 season.

Established himself in first team and made his first appearance at Twickenham in 1990 Cup Final against Gloucester, scoring a try. He suffered a thigh injury at the start of the 1991-92 season and undertook a successful operation on knee in May 1992. Callard returned to full fitness in the 1992/93 season, mainly playing in the second team as a popular and skilful full back, and as understudy to Jonathan Webb. Now he is the undisputed full back for Bath with a tremendous record.

Callard was the England full back in the victorious team against the All Blacks, and also versus Scotland and Ireland. Called out to South Africa tour in 1994, where he received horrendous injuries to his head, nearly losing his sight. Now recovered he is captain of Bath's successful Sevens team who won both the Middlesex Save and Prosper Sevens and the Welsh Worthington Sevens for the Snelling Trophy during 1994. Despite his steady performances for England, Callard was overlooked for the England First XV. In the 1995 World Cup squad, playing for England once and on the bench five times. Jonathan had a superb season for Bath in 1996/97, seeming even safer under the high ball and giving a significant contribution in attack. Late call up for England's Argentina Tour 1997.

Mike Catt

Position: Fly-half/Centre
Date of Birth: 17 September 1971
Place of Birth: Port Elizabeth, South Africa
Height: 5' 10"
Weight: 13st 8lbs

Mike Catt joined Bath during the 1992/93 season. A sudden arrival at Bath brought this outstanding Eastern Province player into immediate prominence at centre and at fly half. His first team debut against Nottingham (5 December 1992) followed by appearance against Richmond.

He featured in a stronger Bath side against London Irish in Jan 1993, scoring two tries to establish himself as understudy to Stuart Barnes. Toured Australia with England Under-21, scoring a try in the Test victory in Sydney. This heralded a meteoric rise up the England ranks, culminating in a two minute appearance in the final international of the 1993/94 season as replacement, thus gaining his first cap, which he followed by making the England squad for South Africa, in the summer of 1994. Catt was on the bench for England versus Rumania and Canada, replacing Hull at full back in the latter game making such an impression (scoring two tries) that he was picked in that position for England's first game in the Five Nations, and held his place both at home and in the World Cup.

After a disappointing time in South Africa, Mike had a difficult beginning to the season, both at fly half for Bath and fly half/full back for England before showing his true class for Bath in the latter part of the 1995/96 season. Attended part of England tour of Argentina 1997, then called up by the British Lions to his native South Africa, following injury to Grayson. Played well and selected as replacement for second test, with full selection for the final test. Mike Catt will always be remembered as the country's first professional rugby player.

SECTION 4 – ALLIED DUNBAR PREMIERSHIP

Philip De Glanville
Position: Centre
Date of Birth: 01 October 1968
Place of Birth: Loughborough
Height: 5' 11"
Weight: 13st 6lbs

Educated at Bryanston School, Dorset, Durham University and Oxford University, and formerly employed at Cow & Gate, Trowbridge. De Glanville has represented England Students, England Under-21s and England B and England. He joined Bath in the summer of 1990 as first choice partner for Guscott after Simon Halliday's departure to Harlequins at the end of 1990. He scored try in the Pilkington Cup Final and then toured New Zealand with England B, appearing in both Tests, scoring a try in the second before going off injured. He has since developed into a most accomplished centre. De Glanville gained another B international cap against the South Africans and then a full England cap as replacement against the Springboks seven days later. His second cap, also as a replacement, came against Wales.

De Glanville was chosen for the England tour of Canada but came home with a shoulder injury before the Tests, which deprived him of a Lions tour as replacement. He was then relegated to the bench for most of 1994/95 following the return of Jeremy Guscott but made striking contributions when replacing Tony Underwood against Canada and Carling against Argentina (in the World Cup). He was then first choice in the England versus Italy and England versus Western Samoa games in the World Cup. He became the captain of Bath for the 1995/96 and 1996/97 seasons and was then appointed England Captain in November 1996.

Ieuan Evans
Position: Wing
Date of Birth: 21 March 1964
Place of Birth: Capel Dewi
Height: 5' 10"
Weight: 13st 4lbs

Awarded MBE in 1996 for services to rugby. Joined Bath from Llanelli on 15 August 1997 on a two year contract. Ieuan has achieved a record breaking seventy-one caps for Wales with twenty-eight games as captain. He has scored a record breaking 33 tries for Wales and has made seven appearances for the British Lions.

He is a member of the elite band of Triple Lions Tourists, having played in Australia 1989, New Zealand 1993 and South Africa 1997. He has played in all three world cups having made over seventy Test Career International Caps scoring 33 tries.

Jeremy Guscott
Position: Centre
Date of Birth: 07 July 1965
Place of Birth: Bath
Height: 6' 1"
Weight: 13st 10lbs

Educated at Ralph Allen School, Bath, and joined Bath mini-rugby section at the age of seven, graduating through all eleven stages and making his first team debut in 1985. Jeremy made his England debut against Rumania in 1989, scoring three tries. Since that time, his international and club career has gone from strength to strength.

He has an outstanding tour with British Lions to South Africa in 1997 and was selected for England v Australia later than same year but requested withdrawal from consideration suffering from fatigue after so many arduous games. In the event, Guscott broke his left arm in the third South African Test which delayed his availability for Bath for some time. Despite that and other injuries, his Test Career has seen him gain over sixty International Caps.

SECTION 4 – ALLIED DUNBAR PREMIERSHIP

Martin Haag
Position: Lock
Date of Birth: 28 July 1965
Place of Birth: Chelmsford
Height: 6' 5"
Weight: 16st 7lbs

After representative honours with England Schools and Cornwall, Martin Haag joined Bath in 1987, establishing a first team place in the 1990/91 season Courage League team. Haag was the Bath 'Player of the Year' in 1991 and gained England B caps against Spain and Ireland B in 1992, before being selected for the New Zealand tour, winning third B cap in second Test. Haag has gained a reputation as a Sevens star, playing in Bath's Sevens which won the Save & Prosper and the Welsh Snelling Sevens, as well as in Malaysia and elsewhere. He has performed outstanding work for the last three seasons in the continued absence of Andy Reed, making more first team appearances last year (twenty-nine) than anyone else. This strong and committed Lock forward was then named Bath 'Player of the Year' again. He has continued to be absolutely invaluable to Bath and England during 1995/96, and was a key member of the England tour Argentina in 1997.

John Mallett
Position: Prop
Date of Birth: 28 May 1970
Place of Birth: Lincoln
Height: 6' 1"
Weight: 16st

With the ability to play tight or loose head prop, Mallett is a key member of the Bath squad. Educated at Millfield School, West London Institute of Higher Education and Bath University, he toured Australia with England Schools, before going to Canada with England Students. He was captain of the successful England Colts side which included Steve Ojomoh, and was later selected for England Emerging players v All Blacks at Gloucester and toured South Africa with the full England Squad in 1994. Mallet was a regular member of England 'A', followed by a call up for the 1995 World Cup squad, where he gained his cap as replacement against Western Samoa. Recurrent injuries meant that he was unable to turn out for the first team for much of the 1992/93 season, and the whole of 1995/96 season. Though he is now fit and on the fringes of the England squad.

Andy Nicol
Position: Scrum Half
Date of Birth: 12 March 1971
Place of Birth: Dundee
Height: 5' 11"
Weight: 13st 4lbs

Educated at Dundee High School and University of Abertay, Dundee, Andy began his rugby career at the age of six with Panmure Mini Rugby Club in Dundee. He played three seasons for Scotland Schools, and captained the Under-19's before progressing to Under-21's, before earning a Scotland B cap in March 1991, scoring Scotland B's only try.

Toured North America with Scotland in 1991 and joined Bath in 1994. Nicol's early career was dogged by injury to his knee, and it was only at the beginning of the 1995/96 season that he was back fully fit and playing his full part in the First XV squad. He has had ten caps for Scotland, the first being in January 1992 (seven for Scotland and twenty-five for England) and was a replacement on the British Lions tour to New Zealand in 1993. Andy captained the Scotland team on tour to the South Seas in 1993. Additionally, he played for the World XV in 1992 in New Zealand to celebrate the NZRFU Centenary, and for the Barbarians in the Hong Kong 7s in 1992 and on their Easter tour in 1994.

Unfortunately, his injury prevented him from taking any part in the 1995 World Cup. After a blinding start at Bath for the 1995/96 season, Andy competed for first team scrum half position with Ian Sanders. He was delighted to be back with Scotland, touring the southern hemisphere with them in 1996. Andy made a very brief appearance in the Cardiff v Bath European quarter final (1996), but was once again dogged by injury. Scotland captain for tour of Zimbabwe and South Africa 1997.

SECTION 4 – ALLIED DUNBAR PREMIERSHIP

Eric Peters
Position: FL/8
Date of Birth: 28 January 1969
Place of Birth: Glasgow
Height: 6' 5"
Weight: 16st 6lbs

Captain of Cambridge University 1992-93, led the combined Oxford-Cambridge side on tour to South Africa in the summer of 1993 before joining Bath. A talented Sevens player, he is an invaluable member of Bath's successful Sevens squad. A natural footballer, whose skill has quickly been recognised by Scotland. After a successful game with Scotland 'A', he was selected for his first international, against Canada in January 1995. From then on, a regular with the Scotland team, culminating in his trip with the Scots to the World Cup.

Recently he has had to fight for a place in Bath's first team and has usually lost out to Ojomoh and Robinson. However, he is a regular for Scotland, touring the southern hemisphere in 1995/96 and was part of the Scotland mini tour of Zimbabwe and South Africa

Nigel Redman

Position: Lock
Date of Birth: 16 August 1964
Place of Birth: Cardiff
Height: 6' 4"
Weight: 17st 2lbs

Joined Bath from Weston-Super-Mare after winning England Colts caps and was controversially selected for Bath's first John Player Cup Final against Bristol in May 1984 at the age of nineteen. His first England cap came against Australia in November of that year, still a teenager, and now has twenty caps, despite his international career being spent in shadow of Ackford and Dooley.

Selected for England World Cup squad in 1987 and again in 1991. Selected for tour of Canada summer 1993 and named in England preliminary squad at start of 1993-94 season. Restored to the full England team in 1993-94 and made a great impact, being named RFU 'Player of the Year'.

Redman was a member of the England squad for South Africa in the summer of 1994, where he made an outstanding contribution. A great line-out jumper and most athletic forward, his international career being sadly slowed by the emergence of Bayfield and Johnson. With Martin Haag, he has been the mainstay of the Bath second row. 'Ollie' was appointed Assistant Coach at Bath, in February 1997 and at age of thirty-two, he was selected for the England tour of Argentina in 1997, then came an astonishing mid-tour call-up for the British Lions in South Africa, following an injury to Weir, crowned with a Lions captaincy and a win versus provincial side Free State.

SECTION 4 – ALLIED DUNBAR PREMIERSHIP

Richard Webster
Position: Flanker
Date of Birth: 09 July 1967
Place of Birth: Morriston
Height: 6' 2"
Weight: 17st

Richard joined Bath in 1996 from Salford Rugby League Club. He first attracted attention as an outstanding Welsh Youth international in 1985/86, winning six caps. Whilst enjoying a summer of rugby in Australia the following year, he was awarded his first full cap against Australia in the play-off game of the 1987 World Cup when Wales won 21-22. A persistent knee injury kept him sidelined from international progress until 1990, when he played against the Centenary Barbarians. His Five Nations debut was Ireland 15 v Wales 16 in 1992, then Wales 15 v Scotland 12 in 1992 when he scored a try. As a Flanker at Swansea, he helped them beat Australia 6-21 at St Helens in November 1992. Richard then switched to Rugby League, joining Salford in October 1993. He played five times for Wales Rugby League between 1993 and 1996, scoring a try in his first game to win the game against France 16-15 in October 1993.

'Webby' has been an instant success at Bath, both on and off the field. He re-appeared in Welsh Union contention with a Wales Emerging cap v South Africa 'A' in December 1996.

Bedford

Ground
Goldington Road,
Goldington
Bedford
MK40 3NF

Colours
Shirts: Sky Blue, Royal Blue and Navy Blue hoops
Shorts: Navy Blue
Change Shirts: Sky Blue and Navy Blue hoop
Shorts: Navy Blue

History
Founded: 1886
Number of International Players: 24
Total Number of individual caps: 135
First capped player: Frederick Brooks, England v South Africa at Crystal Palace, 8 December 1906
Most capped player: (36) Budge Rogers (England 34, Lions 2) (1961-69)
Most tries in tests: 5 in 13 tests by William Steele (Scotland) (1971-74).
Steele's first cap in 1969 came as a Langholm player and his last 9 tests came as a London Scottish player.
Most points in tests: 18 in 13 tests by William Steele (Scotland)
Most club appearances: 485 Budge Rogers

Bedford lifted the inaugural Allied Dunbar Premiership Two title (1997/98), securing promotion to Allied Dunbar One. They also qualified for the Cheltenham and Gloucester Cup final where they narrowly lost to Gloucester after a terrific cup run in defeating first division teams, Richmond, Bristol and Sale.

SECTION 4 – ALLIED DUNBAR PREMIERSHIP

Prominent Players
Joe Ewens
Position: Centre
Date of Birth: 16 December 1977
Place of Birth: Bristol
Height: 6' 0"
Weight: 13st

Joe started playing rugby at Colston's School, Bristol, and has been capped ten times at under-16 and under-18 level achieving the England under-18 captaincy. He then progressed to be capped by England under 21's and the England 'A' team in 1996.

Ewens has played at Clifton Club and appeared briefly, with singular success in the Bath v Wigan Challenge Game at Twickenham. He is an outstanding prospect and a good all round performer at club level, with youth on his side and if he continues to grow in stature as a player, more international recognition may be around the corner.

Alistair Murdoch
Position: centre/wing
Date of birth: 9 May 1968
Place of birth: Sydney, Australia
Height: 6' 1"
Weight: 14st 7lb

Described by Director of Coaching Paul Turner as 'a pot of gold' soon after his arrival in August 1997, Alistair's season came to a pre-mature end in mid-February when breaking a finger in training. Reportedly underrated in his home country, Alistair 'Doc' Murdoch has incredible pace and is superb at tackling from behind. Yet he is still to play in his favourite position on the wing for Bedford and make it his own. He started his career with New South Wales, making ninety-seven appearances and has two Australian caps to his name as well as Barbarians experience.

Junior Paramore

Position: flanker/No. 8
Date of birth: 18 November 1968
Place of birth: Apia, Western Samoa
Height: 6' 2"
Weight: 16st 7lb

Added the inaugural Allied Dunbar Two Players Player of the Season award for 1997/98 to the Beds Times and Citizen Player of the Year accolade won in the previous season. A real crowd favourite since his arrival at Goldington Road in October 1996, Junior is an intimidating figure renowned for his ability to run with the ball and score crucial tries. Look out for the characteristic grimace when the going gets tough! A Western Samoa international, he started his playing career in New Zealand for Manurewa before converting his talents to Rugby League, representing Hunters Mariners in Australia and Castleford in the UK, before moving to Bedford.

Rory Underwood

Position: Wing
Date of Birth: 19 June 1963
Place of Birth: Middlesbrough
Height: 5' 9"
Weight: 14st

Flight Lieutenant Underwood has achieved everything the game has to offer in a phenomenal career. He left Leicester to reunite with former England manager, Geoff Cooke, at the start of the 1998/99 season and is still a constant threat down the flank. Experience will be essential in Bedford's first season in the top flight since 1989-90.

Underwood started off his career with his hometown club of Middlesbrough where he caught the eye from 1979 until 1983. Leicester brought in his obvious talent in 1983 and Underwood would remain at the midlands club until his transfer to Bedford in 1997. Underwood's honours are numerous in an international rugby career that made his a household name. He represented England 85 times between 1984 and 1996, scoring 49 tries and was a regular in the British Lions set up during the same period. He is a consummate professional and just the type of player who can not only please the fans, but bring the game to more and more people as a household name.

SECTION 4 – ALLIED DUNBAR PREMIERSHIP

Rudolph Straeuli
Position: 8/Flanker/lock
Date of birth: 20 August 1963
Place of birth: Pretoria, South Africa
Height: 6' 5"
Weight: 17st 4lb

Straeuli has been a supreme force as Bedford's number eight, but he is also one of the most versatile players on their books. Rudi recovered from long-term injury to play a prominent role in the second half of the 1997/98 season. Captained South Africa six times making a total of thirty-three appearances, gaining a World Cup winning medal in 1995. He has also represented the South African Barbarians, the Barbarians and the provincial teams of Blue Bulls and Transvaal. At club level, his former teams include Penarth (Wales), Pretoria Harlequins, Cantania & Padova (Italy) and Wanderers (Johannesburg).

Gloucester FC

Ground
Kingsholm
Kingsholm Road
Gloucester
GL1 3AX
Stadium Capacity: 10,800

Colours
Shirts: Cherry & White stripes
Shorts: Black
Change Shirts: Black, Cherry & White stripes
Shorts: Black

History
Founded: 1873
Number of International Players: 48
Total number of individual caps: 270
First capped player: Frank Stout, England v Wales at Newport, 9 Jan 1897.
Most capped player: (29) Tom Voyce (England 27, Great Britain 2) (1920-26).
Most tries in tests: 9 in 8 tests by Arthur Hudson (1906-10).
Most points in tests: 27 in 8 tests by Arthur Hudson (1906-10).

Prominent Players
Philippe Saint-Andre
Position: Wing
Date of Birth: 19 April 1967
Place of Birth: Romans, France
Height: 5' 11"
Weight: 14st 6lbs

This tricky and very experienced French winger is the cornerstone of the Gloucester team from an attacking point of view, having scored over 100 points during the last two seasons. Saint-Andre has well over seventy Test Career International Caps for France and had scored in excess of 30 tries for in country in his international career. He in one of the most respected wingers in the Allied Dunbar Premiership and at the age of thirty-two, he still boasts a tremendous turn of pace.

SECTION 4 – ALLIED DUNBAR PREMIERSHIP

Steve Ojomoh
Position: 8/Flanker
Date of Birth: 25 May 1970
Place of Birth: Benin City, Nigeria
Height: 6' 3"
Weight: 16st 9lbs

Educated at West Buckland School, Devon, where he distinguished himself as an athlete. Applying his speed and agility to rugby, he represented England Schools (touring Australia), England Colts and South West Under-21s. Steve joined Bath in 1989, establishing a first team place during the 1990/91 season. He then switched to blind-side flanker, making nineteen appearances with four tries in 1991/92. Ojomoh then took part in the League clincher and Cup Final in the same season before being selected for B tour to New Zealand when Wasps' Dean Ryan pulled out. He was then chosen for second test of the tour and scored a try.

Ojomoh has come to prominence as a utility back row forward, now playing blindside or at number 8. He toured Canada in 1993 with England, appearing in both tests and was named in England's preliminary squad for 1993/94 after gaining his first full England cap against Ireland in February 1992. He went to South Africa on the 1994 tour and played in both Tests (being a replacement in the first), but had to spend another season with Bath battling it out for the back row places.

He found himself on the bench for England for most of the Five Nations' games in 1996, coming on as replacement for Dean Richards in the Calcutta Cup game. He went on to be selected for the England World Cup squad, gaining caps against Argentina, Western Samoa and France.

Harlequins FC

Ground
The Stoop Memorial Ground
Langhorn Drive
Twickenham
TW2 7SX
Stadium Capacity: 9,000 All seated

Colours
Shirts: Magenta, French Grey, Chocolate Brown, Light Blue, Black and Light Green
Shorts: White
Change: None

History
Founded 1866
Number of International Players: 97
Total number of individual caps: 738
First capped player: 3 January 1891, William Leake, England v Wales.
Most capped player: (69) Will Carling (England 68, British Lions 1) (1988-97).
Carling's first 4 caps were as a Durham University player.
Most tries in tests: 13 in 69 tests by Will Carling (1988-97).
Most points in tests: 138 in 19 tests by Bob Hiller (1968-72).

Prominent Players
Rory Jenkins
Position: Flanker
Date of Birth: 29 June 1970
Place of Birth: Leicester
Height: 6ft 2 1/2in
Weight: 16st 10lb

Educated at Oundle and Cambridge University, Jenkins made his debut for Harlequins in September 1994 against Lansdowne. This tall and athletic Flanker, started his career at Brixham and represented Devon Colts before gaining international recognition with England U19 and England U21 caps. Rory was selected for England Students and Cambridge University during his student days before starting out with London Irish and gaining a call up for an Emerging England team. Jenkins soon followed that up with an England A call-up and currently stands strong in the Harlequins line-up and is one of their most important players.

SECTION 4 – ALLIED DUNBAR PREMIERSHIP

Jason Leonard
Position: Prop
Date of Birth: 14 August 1968
Place of Birth: Barking
Height: 5ft 10ins
Weight: 17st 7lbs

Educated at Warren Comprehensive, Leonard is a traditional, hard-working Prop forward who plays with grit and determination. In a glittering career which started at Barking before hitting the big-time with Saracens, Leonard has represented England at Colts, England B and at full international level as well as representing the British Lions. He is a big character in the Harlequins set up and always gives one hundred percent.

Dan Luger
Position: Wing
Date of Birth: 11 January 1975
Place of Birth: Chiswick
Height: 6ft 1in
Weight: 14st 2lb

Dan Luger at Latymer Upper School and Manchester University, he is a hard-working, pacey Winger who made his debut for Harlequins in September 1996 against West Hartlepool, having represented Richmond and Orrell. Luger first started to be noticed when representing Middlesex Schools, Colts and U21, before progressing on to London Colts, U21 and then onto the international stage. 'Dan the man' ran the wing with England Students, England U21 and England A before representing England at the highest level. He still has a lot more to offer both his country and his club.

David Officer
Position: Outside centre/Full back
Date of Birth: 9th May 1973
Place of Birth: Aberdeen
Height: 6ft 2in
Weight: 14st 4lb

David Officer is a much travelled and most highly rated player who can play at Outside Centre or at full back. He was educated at the Montrose Academy and the University of Edinburgh, the latter of which he represented before turning out for Heriots FP, Currie, Burnside and Christchurch, New Zealand.

This quick and agile Scot made his Harlequin debut on the 5 September 1998 v Leicester at the age of 25 having represented Scotland at under-21 level, Scotland A and the full Scotland squad on their tour to Australia in 1998. David has also played for Scottish Universities and Scottish Students Caledonia.

Keith Wood
Position: Hooker
Date of Birth: 27 January 1972
Place of Birth: Limerick
Height: 6ft
Weight: 17st

Educated at St Munchins College, this strong and talented Irish hooker is one of the best players that Ireland have produced in that position over the last few years. He started off his career in the middle of the scrum for Garryowen and went on to represent Munster before making his Harlequin debut in 1996 against Gloucester.

Internationally recognised, Wood has turned out for his country on numerous occasions and at all levels from Ireland under-21 to Ireland A before making his full international debut for Ireland. Wood also went on to be selected for the British Lions and remains a part of the Irish international scene as well as becoming a stalwart of the Harlequin side. His dependable hooking and quick feet have earned his a good reputation and standing within the game.

SECTION 4 - ALLIED DUNBAR PREMIERSHIP

Leicester

Ground
Welford Road Ground
Aylestone Road
Leicester
LE2 7TR
Stadium Capacity: 16,500

Colours
Shirts: Scarlet, Green & White hooped stripes
Shorts: White
Change Shirts: Navy with Scarlet Green and White band
Shorts: White

History
Founded: 1880
Number of International Players: 71
Total number of individual caps: 604
First capped player: Jack Miles, England v Wales at Swansea, 10 January 1903.
Most capped player: (91) Rory Underwood (England 85, Lions 6) (1984-96).
Most tries in tests: Rory Underwood (England 49, Lions 1) (1984-96).
Most points in tests: 240 in 24 tests by Dusty Hare (1978-84). Hare played in his first test match as a Nottingham player.

Club Honours
Courage League Champions: 1987/8, 1994/5
Runners Up: 1993/4, 1995/6
European Cup Finalists: 1996/7
Pilkington Cup Winners: 1992/3, 1996/7
Finalists: 1988/9, 1993/4, 1995/6
John Player Cup Winners: 1978/9, 1979/80, 1980/1
Finalists: 1977/8, 1982/3
Middlesex VII's Winners: 1994/5

Prominent players
Neil Back
Position: Flanker
Date of Birth: 16 January 1969
Place of Birth: Coventry
Height: 5' 10"
Weight: 14st

Neil Back in one of the countries most experienced Flankers and is a firm favourite with the Welford Road crown. The Coventry born pacey Forward has represented England in over twenty International tests and has scored some vital tries, not only for his country, but for his club. With well over two hundred points for Leicester in his first two seasons, he remains a threat to all defences including the best that the world has to offer.

Richard Cockerill
Position: Hooker
Date of Birth: 16 December 1970
Place of Birth: Rugby
Height: 5' 10"
Weight: 17st

Richard Cockerill was born in Rugby and born to play rugby! With well over twenty Test Career International Caps for England under his belt, he is a very experienced asset in the Leicester side.

A tough and fast hooker, Cockrill also does well in open play averaging around 4 tries per season,at club level, which is a cracking recorded for a player who spends most of his time in the middle of the scrummage pack. He has also come up with some important and timely scores for his country.

SECTION 4 – ALLIED DUNBAR PREMIERSHIP

Martin Corry
Position: 8/Flanker
Date of Birth: 12 October 1973
Place of Birth: Birmingham
Height: 6ft 5ins
Weight: 16st 1lb

This tall, hard-hitting and versatile 'Brummy' is a big player for both club and country. With several Test Career International Caps under his belt for England, he has secured his place in the Leicester line-up and grown in stature over the last few seasons. He gets his fair share of the points from both Flanking and at number 8, the latter position being his best in many pundits opinions. Standing at 6ft 5ins he is the perfect build for the 8 spot.

Darren Garforth
Position: Prop
Date of Birth: 09 April 1966
Place of Birth: Coventry
Height: 5' 10"
Weight: 18st 9lbs

Darren Garforth is a tough, strong and weighty prop forward, whose talents have led him to International recognition with over twenty first class international test appearances for his country England. Going forward he is extremely bulky and hard to stop and is often in the forefront of rucks and mauls. He is a big player for Leicester in more ways than one and is never afraid to get 'stuck in' for the cause!

Will Greenwood
Position: Centre
Date of Birth: 20 October 1972
Place of Birth: Blackburn
Height: 6' 4"
Weight: 15st 12lbs

This twenty-seven-year-old Centre from the north-west has impressed many with his running and scoring abilities in the Allied Dunbar Premiership and at International level. He is a well-paced, quick-thinking player with good hands and passing ability. He has represented and scored for England in tests and is regularly on the score sheet for his club.

Martin Johnson
Position: Lock Forward
Date of Birth: 09 March 1970
Place of Birth: Solihull
Height: 6' 6"
Weight: 18st 7lbs

Midlands born Martin Johnson is a front row lock forward of the highest calibre. He is a tall and awkward player who is very strong in the scrum and a tough tackler. His obvious talent has been recognised International level with well over fifty Test Career International Caps for England.

At rucks and mauls he is a very handy player to have on your side with the power and strength to defend relentlessly and a good 'Rugby brain' that can start forward attacks in motion.

Tim Stimpson
Position: Fullback
Date of Birth: 10 September 1973
Place of Birth: Liverpool
Height: 6ft 3ins
Weight: 15st 12lbs

Tom Stimpson is a very exciting player with pace and agility. Coming from Merseyside, this quick-witted and talented back has experienced test matches with England and is an excellent scorer at club level. He has the skill and determination to score tries and turn matches around, while his kick ability in front of goal has helped his score well over six hundred points in his English club career.

SECTION 4 – ALLIED DUNBAR PREMIERSHIP

Joel Stransky
Position: Fly Half
Date of Birth: 16 July 1967
Place of Birth: Pietermaritzburg, S Africa
Height: 5ft 10ins
Weight: 13st 7lbs

Joel Stransky is one of his clubs most important players and is in established International Fly Half for his native South Africa. He has skill in abundance and is probably the finest player in his position playing the Allied Dunbar Premiership. In his English club career, he has raced past the 500 points mark, and has kicked over a hundred penalties and almost over a hundred conversion kicks.

London Irish

Ground
The Avenue
Sunbury On Thames
Middlesex
TW16 5EQ
Stadium Capacity: 6,800

Colours
Shirts: Green
Shorts: White
Change Shirts: Black/Ecru
Shorts: Black

History
Founded: 1898
Number of International Players: 49
Total number of individual caps: 339
First capped player: Standish Cagney (Ireland v Wales at Belfast), 14 March 1925.
Most capped player: (36) Ken Kennedy (Ireland 32, British Lions 4) (1966-75). Kennedy also appeared in 5 tests as a Queens University player and another 8 as a CIYMS player.
Most tries and points in tests: Hugo MacNeill in 16 tests (7 tries, 28 points) (1986-88). MacNeill also appeared in 9 tests as a Dublin University player scoring 3 tries and 15 points, 13 tests as an Oxford University player scoring 3 points, plus another 2 for Blackrock College.

SECTION 4 – ALLIED DUNBAR PREMIERSHIP

Prominent players
Rob Hardwick
Position: Prop
Date of Birth: 29 March 1969
Place of Birth: Kenilworth
Height 6' 0"
Weight: 18st 5lbs

Rob Hardwick is tough and gritty player who bounced back from a career-threatening knee-ligament injury that caused a two and a half year absence from the game. Was encouraged to help with the Coventry Colts and this gave him the enthusiasm and motivation to beat the injury.

Rob forced his way to the fringes of the England squad and won his only England cap to date as a replacement playing against Italy at Twickenham in November 1996. Hardwick then toured Argentina in the summer of 1997 with England, although the management's preference for Bath players meant that he missed out to Kevin Yates in both Tests.

Malcolm O'Kelly
Position: Lock
Date of Birth: 19 July 1974
Place of Birth: Chelmsford
Height: 6' 7"
Weight: 16st - 2lbs

This tall and strong Irish Lock forward was born in Chelmsford but has represented Ireland at International Test level nine times although he is certainly young enough to add to that tally as his continues to impress with his strong league performances.

Conor O'Shea
Position: Fullback
Date of Birth: 21 October 1970
Place of Birth: Limerick
Height: 6' 2"
Weight: 15st 12lbs

Conor O'Shea is a well accomplished Fullback who is not only solid as a rock for London Irish, but also for his Country at International test level. He is a good all-round point scorer for club and country and regularly chips in with important Penalties and Conversion kicks.

Brendan Venter
Position: Centre
Date of Birth: 29 December 1969
Place of Birth: Johannesburg, S Africa
Height: 6' 1"
Weight: 13st 7lbs

Brendan Venter is and athletic and experience campaigner, who has certainly hit it off with the fans of London Irish. The South African born Centre is a regular in the side and has many international caps to boot. Having arrived at The Avenue just last season, he is already showing that he can kick it in the Allied Dunbar Premiership.

Niall Woods
Position: Wing
Date of Birth: 21 June 1971
Place of Birth: Dublin
Height: 6' 0"
Weight: 12st 13lbs

Niall is a Irishman through and through, taking great pride in his caps for his country at all levels. He is very quick and hard to defend against going forwards and is a pretty reliable kicker of penalties and conversions. In his English league career, Niall had scored well over five hundred points, and had ran some very impressive tries of late.

SECTION 4 – ALLIED DUNBAR PREMIERSHIP

James Brown
Position: Fly Half
Date of Birth: 8 December 1977
Place of Birth: Solihull
Height: 5' 8"
Weight: 12st 8lbs

Born in Solihull and educated at Millfield School. Has been capped at Schools 18 and 16 Groups. James joined the club in May 1996 and toured Australia with England Under-21s in the summer of 1997, having made four appearances for the Coventry first team before joining London Irish. He is a player of the future and many expect him to be a shining star to come. He certainly has an eye for a try and is continually improving as a quality kicker.

London Scottish

Ground

The Stoop Memorial Ground
Langhorn Drive
Twickenham
TW2 7SX
Stadium Capacity: 9,000 All seated

Colours

Shirts: Blue
Shorts: Blue
Change Shirts: 'Heather'
Shorts: Blue

History

Founded: 1878
Number of International Players: 141
Total number of individual caps: 874
First capped player: Fraser Gore, Scotland v Ireland 18 February 1882.
Most capped player: (42) Alastair McHarg (Scotland) (1968-79). McHarg's first two caps came as a West of Scotland player.
Most tries in tests: 8 in 23 tests by Derek White (Scotland) (1989-92). White's first 18 caps came whilst with Gala Academy scoring 3 tries.
Most points in tests: (157) Gavin Hastings (129 in 14 tests for Scotland and 28 in 3 tests for Lions) (1989-90). Hastings began and ended his test career as a Watsonians player, gaining 50 caps (3 for the Lions) and scoring 576 points including 14 tries whilst with that club.

Prominent Players
Paul Burnell

Position: Prop
Date of Birth: 29 September 1965
Place of Birth: Edinburgh
Height: 6' 0"
Weight: 17st 5lbs

Paul Burnell has been around for quite some time now and has managed to represent Scotland and the British Lions on over fifty occasions, leading the front row and using his considerable stature both defensively and offensively. Never the biggest scorer of tries, he has however scored a try at test level. An important player for London Scottish, his experience and determination can give them a great advantage in the scrummage.

SECTION 4 – ALLIED DUNBAR PREMIERSHIP

Jannie De Beer
Position: Fly Half
Date of Birth: 22 April 1971
Place of Birth: Welkom, S Africa
Height: 6' 0"
Weight: 13st 9lbs

Jannie De Beer is a Fly half of top quality both for London Scottish and his country South Africa. He racked up 79 points for the Springbok in just seven appearances and also has a good scoring record for London Scottish, approaching two hundred English league career points. He has great awareness and is a skilled Penalty kicker.

Paul Johnstone
Position: Prop
Date of Birth: 16 October 1970
Place of Birth: Bulawayo, Zimbabwe
Height: 6' 0"
Weight: 17st 5lbs

When it comes to hard-hitting and tough prop forwards, Paul Johnstone is a fine example. He has established himself in the London Scottish scrum along side Paul Burnell and has brought more great International Test experience to the side with over forty caps for Zimbabwe. Although he is a skilled and agile forward, he doesn't tend to get forward enough, a fact that is reflected in his scoring record, but nevertheless, his stature and determination have made him a worthy prop of the highest quality.

Ian McAusland
Position: Fullback
Date of Birth: 15 January 1976
Place of Birth: Sydney, Australia
Height: 5' 10"
Weight: 13st 4lbs

An amazing surname for a player who hails from down under and plays for a predominantly Scottish side! Ian McAusland is a firm favourite with the fans at The Stoop Memorial Ground and is a hard-working and talented performer with a real talent in front of goal. In his English league career, he has kicked well over two hundred points in little over two full seasons, although full International recognition has eluded him thus far.

SECTION 4 – ALLIED DUNBAR PREMIERSHIP

Newcastle Falcons

Ground
Kingston Park
Brunton Road
Kenton Bank Foot
Newcastle
NE13 8AF
Stadium Capacity: 6,400

Colours
Shirts: White with irregular Black hoops, Black collar
Shorts: Black
Change Shirts: Black with White hoops, Black collar
Shorts: Black

History
Founded: 1995 (Gosforth formed in 1877)
Number of International Players: 19
Total number of individual caps: 158
First capped player: Arthur Smith, Scotland v Ireland in Dublin, 1 March 1958. Smith had previously played test rugby at Cambridge University.
Most capped player: (23) Roger Uttley (England 19, Lions 4) (1973-79). Uttley also made his last four test appearances as a Wasps player.
Most tries in tests: 4 in 17 tests by Peter Dixon (1973-78). Dixon made his first 8 test appearances (including 3 for the Lions) as a Harlequins player, scoring 1 try worth 3 points.
Most points in tests: 16 in 17 tests by Peter Dixon (1973-78).

Prominent Players
Rob Andrew
Position: Fly Half
Date of Birth: 18 February 1963
Place of Birth: Richmond, Yorkshire
Height: 5' 9"
Weight: 12st 8lbs

What can you say about Rob Andrew? He is an extremely talented player, a leader, a quality kicker, and ingenious user of the ball and is a household name. With over seventy International test caps for England the British Lions and over four hundred test points, Rob Andrew is a modern rugby legend, who has shone wherever he has played and continues to do so now, with a strong and athletic Newcastle team.

His international career spanned great heights and his English league scoring record in exemplary with over 1300 career point, most of which have come from some for of kicking. He is of course, much more than a goal-scorer. His overall play is sometimes dazzling. He still has quick feet and a real intelligence when passing and setting up plays. He is a hero in Newcastle just as he is all over the country and indeed the world!

Garath Archer
Position: Lock
Date of Birth: 15 December 1974
Place of Birth: South Shields
Height: 6' 6"
Weight: 18st 7lbs

A Geordie born lad who has achieved quite a lot in his short career. Garath Archer is a tremendous Lock forward with height, strength, presence and agility that has been recognised at International Test level for England. He is also quite a high scoring first rower, having over seventy career points to his name.

SECTION 4 – ALLIED DUNBAR PREMIERSHIP

Gary Armstrong
Position: Scrum Half
Date of Birth: 30 September 1966
Place of Birth: Edinburgh
Height: 5' 8"
Weight: 13st 8lbs

Armstrong is a key player in the Geordie side and is an experienced and renowned Scrum half. With over forty-five test caps for Scotland and over two hundred and fifty career points in the English league, Gary is an all-rounder, who links well with his back line and with Rob Andrew is a play-maker of some talent. This quick and fluid Scot is the unsung hero of the Geordie Rugby revolution and still has a good few seasons in him yet.

Ross Nesdale
Position: Hooker
Date of Birth: 30 July 1968
Place of Birth: Feilding, New Zealand
Height: 5' 10"
Weight: 16st 2lbs

Ross Nesdale is a well-respected Hooker who has represented Ireland at test level even though he hails from New Zealand. With great balance and a turn of pace, he is also quite a high scoring hooker, with 13 tries in his first couple of seasons in the Allied Dunbar league. He leads the front row of the scrummage with skill and flair breaks quickly into attack areas.

Inga Tuigamala
Position: Winger/Centre
Date of Birth: 4 September 1969
Place of Birth: Faleasiu, W Samoa
Height: 5' 10"
Weight: 17st 4lbs

Inga Tuigamala has got it all! He is big enough to look after himself on the pitch, he is pacey enough to out run defences and take half chances to break and he is skilled enough to link up with the rest of the back to play good attacking rugby. He has over twenty International Test caps with New Zealand and Western Samoa and has a good scoring record in his time in the English league.

Tony Underwood
Position: Wing
Date of Birth: 17 February 1969
Place of Birth: Poh, Malaysia
Height: 5' 9"
Weight: 13st 7lbs

Like his brother Rory, Tony Underwood is a household name and a very experience player. He is a Winger of immense skill and pace and has proved it at the highest of levels. With twenty-seven appearances for England and the British Lions at test level, Tony has not quite achieved the renown afforded to his older brother, but nevertheless he has carved his own name in the annals of Rugby History.

SECTION 4 – ALLIED DUNBAR PREMIERSHIP

Northampton RFC

Ground
Franklins Gardens
Weedon Road
Northampton
NN5 5BG
Stadium Capacity: 10,000

Colours
Shirts: Black, Green & Gold cross bands Shorts: Black
Change Shirts: Black, broad Green band, small Yellow band
Shorts: Black

History
Founded: 1880
Number of International Players: 57
Total number of individual caps: 499
First capped player: Henry Weston, England v Scotland at Blackheath, 9 March 1901.
Most capped player: (37) Dickie Jeeps (England 24, British Lions 13) (1955-62).
Most tries in tests: (8) Jeff Butterfield (England 5, British Lions 3) (1953-59).
Most points in tests: 133 in 8 tests by Paul Grayson (1995-97).

Prominent Players
Nick Beal
Position: Fullback/Winger
Date of Birth: 02 December 1970
Place of Birth: York
Height: 6' 2"
Weight: 13st 8lbs

Nick Beal is an industrious and versatile back who can play at Fullback or on the wing. He has nine International test caps for England and has scored a couple of tries at that level. A stalwart of the Northampton line-up, he is quick and skilful and is a sound kicker of the ball. In his English league career he has racked up approaching two hundred points and leads the line well.

Matt Dawson
Position: Scrum Half
Date of Birth: 31 October 1972
Place of Birth: Birkenhead
Height: 5' 11"
Weight: 12st 10lbs

This twenty-seven-year-old Scrum half has achieved well over twenty International Test caps for both England and the British Lions and is a real play-maker in the Northampton team. Matt Dawson is a swift handler of the ball and an agile performer week-in week-out. His kicking is solid and his eye for a try continues to grow. In his English League career he has notched close to 300 points, most of which have come from scoring tries.

SECTION 4 – ALLIED DUNBAR PREMIERSHIP

Paul Grayson
Position: Fly Half
Date of Birth: 30 May 1971
Place of Birth: Chorley
Height: 6' 0"
Weight: 12st 7lbs

Paul Grayson is a fine Fly half and an excellent kicker of points both for the clubs that he had represented and for England, whom he has appeared for at all levels including over twenty first class International Tests scoring an average of 14 points per game. He is an impressive point scorer having achieved well over a thousand points in his English league career, most of which have come from penalty kicks although three or four tries per season is not beyond him.

Federico Mendez
Position: Hooker
Date of Birth: 2 August 1972
Place of Birth: Ciudad de Mendoza, Argentina
Height: 6' 0"
Weight: 18st

Mendez is a world renowned Hooker with over thirty Argentina Caps, the first of which came aged eighteen in 1990 v Ireland. He played for World XV in 1991 in the New Zealand Centenary and played in two of the three games. An outstanding player and team man, he came to Northampton via Bath after helping Natal win the Currie Cup and is already a crowd favourite.

Tim Rodber
Position: 8/Flanker
Date of Birth: 2 July 1969
Place of Birth: Richmond, Yorks
Height: 6' 6"
Weight: 16st 7lbs

A vastly experience campaigner, Tim Rodler has over forty International Test caps having represented England and the British Lions. A versatile player, happy at number 8 or as Flanker, he is tall and athletic, getting his fair share of tries. In his English league career Tim has scored quite regularly and is an important player in the Northampton set-up.

Jon Sleightholme

Position: Wing
Date of Birth: 5 August 1972
Place of Birth: Malton
Height: 5' 10"
Weight: 13st 5lbs

Jonathan was educated at Whitgift School, Grimsby and represented the Grimsby Rugby Club which he joined in his early teens. He then moved to Hull Ionians before joining Wakefield. After studying Sports Science and Physical Education at Chester College, he became a postgraduate student in the School of Education at Bath University, where among other things he studied Physical Education, with a view to becoming a teacher on graduating.

He has had representative honours with England Under 19s, Under 21s, England Students and the newly formed Emerging Players and last season with England 'A'. Catapulted into the full England side in the first Five Nations game against France in 1995/96, and has since gone from strength to strength both for Club and Country. He was included in the England Tour of Argentina in 1997.

SECTION 4 – ALLIED DUNBAR PREMIERSHIP

Richmond FC
Ground:
Madejski Stadium
Reading
Berkshire RE2 0FL
Stadium Capacity: 25,000
Colours
Shirts: Old Gold, Red and Black hoops
Shorts: Black
Change Shirts: Old Gold, Red and Black hoops
Shorts: Black
History
Founded: 1861
Number of international Players: 74
Total number of individual caps: 351
First capped player: Dawson Turner, England v Scotland at Edinburgh, 27 March 1871 (the first ever test match).
Most capped player: (23) Chris Ralston (England 22, Lions 1) (1971-75).
Most tries in tests: 4 in 8 tests by Henry Twynam (1879-1884).
Most points in tests: 28 in 11 tests by Nim Hall (1952-55). Hall had also played in 6 previous tests as a St Mary's Hospital and Huddersfield player scoring 11.

Prominent Players
Allan Bateman
Position: Centre
Date of Birth: 6 March 1965
Place of Birth: Maesteg, Wales
Height: 5' 9"
Weight: 14st

Nicknamed 'The Clamp' his quick Welsh Centre has had a cracking career, representing Wales at most levels and gaining 16 full International Test caps for the Welsh and for the British Lions as well as representing Wales at Rugby League. Bateman, who has also acquired great notoriety in Rugby League is one of the most popular players at the Richmond club, who he joined after starting his career at Neath before hitting the headlines in the Nineties with his League performances with Warrington and briefly at Cronulla Sharks in Australia.

His style of play was best summed up by the Daily Telegraph's Paul Ackford who said of Bateman:

"His defence is virtually impenetrable, his rugby brain agile and accurate but it is his running which takes the breath away. He never holds the same direction for more than five paces, changing the rhythm a angle of attack constantly."

Richard Butland
Position: Fly Half
Date of Birth: 05 November 1971
Place of Birth: Cape Town, S Africa
Height: 5' 11"
Weight: 13st

He was born in Cape Town, and has dual nationality, as have his parents. Indeed, his grandfather used to play for Natal. However, the family came to settle in UK eleven years ago and Richard attended Wellington College in Berkshire, which is where he started to develop his rugby.

He has slotted in to the fly half role well, and has made a great impression with his all round game. Following a number of friendly matches, Richard played an important part in the latter half of the 1994/95 season, with eight League and Cup appearances, including the Pilkington Cup Final. He has continued to show his considerable promise and is rapidly developing into a fly half of class and vision. Has represented England Students at Fly Half and England 'A' in 1996.

SECTION 4 – ALLIED DUNBAR PREMIERSHIP

Ben Clarke
Position: 8/Flanker
Date of Birth: 15 April 1968
Place of Birth: Bishop's Stortford
Height: 6' 5"
Weight: 18st

Ben Clarke has matured over the years into a dependable and hard-working forward, who can do a great job at number 8 or as a Flanker. His Test career has taken him to over 40 International caps for England and the British Lions. He is a Kingpin of the Richmond line-up and used his build well in line-outs, with the power and strength to direct rucks and mauls and get forward effectively.

Brian Cusack
Position: Lock
Date of Birth: 11 July 1972
Place of Birth: Waterford, Ireland
Height: 6' 7"
Weight: 17st 6lbs

Brian Cusack was educated at Chongowes Wood School and has played for Bective Rangers, Leinster and Ireland A. He has represented Ireland at Senior and Junior levels in athletics, but has yet to break through to the International scene as a Lock Forward. Currently training for a BA in Accountancy and Finance, this tall and athletic player had developed from a squad player to a forward with an eye for a try.

Agustin Pichot
Position: Scrum Half
Date of Birth: 22 August 1974
Place of Birth: Buenos Aires, Argentina
Height: 5' 9"
Weight: 12st 5lbs

This fast and agile Scrum Half hails from Argentina, whom he has approaching twenty Test caps for. He is an extremely important play-maker in the Richmond side and uses the ball to great effect. In his first season with Richmond, he scored 7 tries in seventeen appearances, but more than that, he brought experience and culture to the side.

Matt Pini
Position: Fullback
Date of Birth: 21 March 1969
Place of Birth: Canberra, Australia
Height: 5' 11"
Weight: 14st 12lbs

The man from 'down under', Matt is a highly experienced campaigner a has lost none of his tempo or pace since being in the Allied Dunbar Premiership. With a handful of International Test caps for Australia and Italy, Pini is a key player in the Richmond set-up. He is a strong runner and a good kicker, who always gives a hundred percent when asked to do a job.

Craig Quinnell
Position: Lock
Date of Birth: 09 July 1975
Place of Birth: Swansea
Height: 6' 6"
Weight: 19st 10lbs

This Welsh Lock Forward has scored three International Test Tries for Wales and has an English League career total of 23 tries which is a great scoring record for a Prop. He uses his size and build to great effect in the scrummage, but he has some speed to him and often links up with play going forward. Defensively, Quinnell is a big player with a tough tackle, but he can also lose his temper in the heat of the battle and does receive the odd card.

SECTION 4 – ALLIED DUNBAR PREMIERSHIP

Barry Williams
Position: Hooker
Date of Birth: 6 January 1974
Place of Birth: Carmarthen
Height: 6' 0"
Weight: 16st 6lbs

Another Welsh giant playing at the Madejski Stadium, Williams is a superb Hooker who links up the backs and is a force going forward. With a dozen International Test caps for Wales and the British Lions, he is vastly experienced for a twenty-five-year-old and a key player for Richmond. He gets forward well and often chips in with a try for his team, but the main asset that Williams brings is enormous potential for the future, with more International recognition just around the corner.

Sale
(Manchester Sale Rugby Club)
Ground
Heywood Road
Brooklands
Sale
Cheshire
M33 3WB
Stadium Capacity: 7,500
Colours
Shirts: Royal Blue & White hoops
Shorts: Royal Blue
History
Founded: 1861
Number of international Players: 18
Total number of individual caps: 169
First capped player: George Isherwood, Great Britain v South Africa at Johannesburg, 6 August 1910.
Most capped player: (30): Peter Stagg (Scotland 27, British Lions 3) (1965-70) and Eric Evans (England 30) (1948-58).
Most tries in tests: 5 in 10 tests by Hal Sever (1936-38), and 5 in 30 tests by Eric Evans (1948-58). Most points in tests: 19 in 10 tests by Hal Sever (1936-38).

Prominent Players
Jos Baxendell
Position: Centre
Date of Birth: 03 December 1972
Place of Birth: Manchester
Height: 6' 0"
Weight: 14st 4lbs
After starting out with Wilmslow at the age of eighteen, Jos Baxendall went on to represent Sheffield before joining Manchester Sale late in 1993. He made his Sale debut in January 1994 versus Otley and had grown in stature ever since. His honours include appearances for The North and England A and he has recently been received full International Test honours with England. While still following his career as a Surveyor, Jos continues to improve and was an English tourist to Argentina in the Summer of 1997 and to the Southern Hemisphere the following year.

SECTION 4 – ALLIED DUNBAR PREMIERSHIP

Phil Greening
Position: Hooker
Date of Birth: 03 October 1975
Place of Birth: Gloucester
Height: 6' 0"
Weight: 17st

Phil Greening made his Sale Debut versus London Irish in 1998 and has worked his way up through International to gain five Test caps for England after representing his country at U16, U18, Colts, U21 and England A. He is a skilled and focused Hooker who should be in with a chance of adding to his International Honours.

Steven Hanley
Position: Winger
Date of Birth: 11 June 1979
Place of Birth: Whitehaven
Height: 6' 4"
Weight: 16st 7lbs

This young lad from Whitehaven has represented England at all levels during his short career. Starting with North Colts and England Colts, he progressed with flying colours to represent Midlands/North U21, England U21 and then a rare Test Cap, in which he scored a try. He made his Sale Debut versus Cardiff in October 1998 and since then has scored 12 tries in his first full season.

Shane Howarth
Position: Fly Half/Fullback
Date of Birth: 8 July 1968
Place of Birth: Auckland, New Zealand
Height: 5' 9"
Weight: 13st 10lbs

This versatile New Zealander started off his career with Auckland Maoris before making the trip over to England to join Manchester Sale. He made his Sale Debut versus Saracens in August 1997 and since the move seems to have rekindled his form and International prospects. He had made ten full International Test appearances for the All-blacks and in 1998 for Wales. He is fast approaching the 500 points mark for Sale.

Jim Mallinder
Position: Fullback
Date of Birth: 16 March 1966
Place of Birth: Halifax
Height: 6' 3"
Weight: 16st

The Manchester Sale Captain has been with the club since 1989, after representing Crossleyans and Roundhay. He made his Sale debut against Northampton in October 1989 and was awarded the club captaincy in 1995. Internationally, Mallinder has caps for England A and 2 caps for England as well as recently representing the Barbarians. He was an English tourist to Argentina in the Summer of 1997.

Dion O'Cuinneagain
Position: Number 8
Date of Birth: 24 May 1972
Place of Birth: Cape Town, S Africa
Height: 6' 3"
Weight: 16st 5lbs

Dion O'Cuinneagain has had an interesting sporting career which not only includes ten full International Test caps for Ireland, but he has also represented South African Universities at the 110 metre hurdles while a Medical student at Stellenbosch University and has played Cricket for Western Province U21.

His Rugby honours include caps for Western Province U21, South African Universities, South Africa in World Sevens (as Captain), Ireland A and full Ireland caps. He was an Irish tourist to South Africa in the Summer of 1998 about a year after making his Sale debut against Wasps in 1997

SECTION 4 – ALLIED DUNBAR PREMIERSHIP

David Rees
Position: Winger
Date of Birth: 15 October 1974
Place of Birth: London
Height: 5' 9"
Weight: 13st 7lbs

A Graphic Design student at Manchester Metropolitan University, David Rees is a skilled athlete and had found success at other sports including Newcastle boys soccer, Northumberland U14 tennis and Northumberland Schools 200 metre.

He made his Sale debut in February 1995 against Broughton Park after representing Northern. His rugby honours include caps at England U21 and England A levels as well as ten full Test caps for, England He made the English touring party to Argentina in the Summer of 1997 and has scored three tries at test level.

Pat Sanderson
Position: Flanker
Date of Birth: 6 September 1977
Place of Birth: Chester
Height: 6' 3"
Weight: 16st 5lbs

Born in Chester in 1977, Pat Sanderson is certainly on top of his game at the moment. The young Flanker had just turned nineteen when he turned out for Manchester Sale, making his debut against Newbridge and since then he has represented an Emerging England side, England A, and has received three Full English test caps. He was an English tourist to Southern Hemisphere in 1998 and continues to push for more International recognition.

Saracens

Ground
Vicarage Road Stadium
Watford
Herts
WD1 8ER
Stadium Capacity: 22,000

Colours
Shirts: Black, (Red & White hoop to sleeve)
Shorts: Black
Change Shirts: Black & White band hoop, small Red band hoop between Red & White hoop, Red collar.
Shorts: Black

History
Founded: 1876
Number of International Players: 10
Total number of individual caps: 32
First capped player: John Steeds, England v Ireland at Twickenham, 11 February 1950.
Most capped player: (7) Paul Wallace (Ireland, 1979-84)
Most tries in tests: 2 in 4 tests by Richard Hill (1997).

Prominent Players
Gregg Botterman
Position: Hooker
Date of Birth: 03 March 1968
Place of Birth: Welwyn Garden City
Height: 5' 11"
Weight: 15st 6lbs

Fast approaching a decade with Saracens, this genial hooker still has the rucking and mauling skills which saw him get a place on the bench for England's Grand Slam decider against Scotland in 1995. Despite his involvement with the pack, Botterman has showed that he is capable of linking with the backs and making forward, attacking runs.

SECTION 4 – ALLIED DUNBAR PREMIERSHIP

Kyran Bracken
Position: Scrum Half
Date of Birth: 22 November 1971
Place of Birth: Dublin
Height: 5' 11"
Weight: 13st 3lbs

This Law graduate from Bristol University who was unlucky to be omitted from this summer's British Lions tour to South Africa. Bracken was very impressive on the England tour to Argentina in 1998, where he showed pace, verve and great passing ability. After that tour he was called in as a replacement for the injured Lions scrum half Robert Howley, and thus fulfiled one of his ambitions in playing for the British Lions. He has well over twenty International test caps and is still young enough and hungry enough to gain more.

Troy Coker
Position: Lock
Date of Birth: 30 May 1963
Place of Birth: Brisbane, Australia
Height: 6' 6"
Weight: 18st

Troy joined the Saracens from the successful Super 12 side ACT Brumbies. Having being capped twenty-seven times for Australia and played for the likes of Queensland as well, he brings a wealth of experience to the squad. He is a powerful figure in the scrummage and can link up well in attack. His high level of experience has stood him in good stead in the Allied Dunbar Premiership and he has become a firm favourite with the Vicarage Road faithful.

Ryan Constable
Position: Centre/Winger
Date of Birth: 20 October 1971
Place of Birth: Durban, S Africa
Height: 6' 0"
Weight: 13st

Constable, who was capped by Australia once against Ireland in 1994, can play either in the centre or on the wing. With such intense competition for places in the Queensland side with World class players such as Tim Horan and Danny Herbert, Ryan sought a new opportunity by coming to London. Queensland released him from his contract to allow him to join Saracens and to link up with his old team-mate Michael Lynagh. Ryan is captain of Australia's Sevens side, and has settled in well to his role with Saracens.

Tony Diprose
Position: 8/Flanker
Date of Birth: 22 September 1972
Place of Birth: Orsett
Height: 6' 5"
Weight: 17st 8lbs

An amazing performance against Harlequins in the Pilkington Cup and in the last nine games of the 1997/98 season, finally ensured Tony earned a well deserved call-up to the England squad for the 1998 summer tour to Argentina. An outstanding scrummager and controller of events in and around the scrum, Tony also easily links up with the backs when required and always seems to be on hand to receive the ball. Given the way he's captained Saracens and England 'A' in the past, it's no wonder that he's a key man in the Saracens team.

SECTION 4 - ALLIED DUNBAR PREMIERSHIP

Danny Grewcock
Position: Lock
Date of Birth: 7 November 1972
Place of Birth: Coventry
Height: 6' 6"
Weight: 17st 7lbs

Danny Grewcock is a Coventry lad born and bred. He served an apprenticeship at Barkers Butts, a feeder club to Coventry, and then helped Coventry to promotion from Division Three and in 1998 into the play-offs where they lost to London Irish. To cap a magnificent year he leapfrogged into the England tour of Argentina where he was capped in the second test. Danny, also played for England Students while studying at Crewe and Alsager College.

Richard Hill
Position: Flanker
Date of Birth: 23 May 1973
Place of Birth: Dormansland
Height: 6' 3"
Weight: 15st 8lbs

A meteoric rise to international rugby in 1998 culminated in Richard's selection for the prestigious British Lions tour to South Africa in the summer. Richard then went on to play against Ireland, France and Wales during the Five Nations Campaign which saw England win the Triple Crown. He has cause to be proud of his performance against Ireland because during the 46-6 win he scored his first England try. This graduate of Brunel University also played in the 1997 World Cup Sevens. Hill is one of the best Flankers in English club rugby and shows great prowess when rucking, mauling, running and his ability to score tries.

Gavin Johnson
Position: Fullback/Winger
Date of Birth: 17 October 1966
Place of Birth: Louis Trichardt, S Africa
Height: 6' 2"
Weight: 14st 7lbs

Gavin Johnson joined Saracens part way through the 1997/98 season and soon settled into the team. A full back that was never afraid to attack from deep and whose touch kicking saw many an eighty-yard punt. He has racked up over ten full International test caps for his native South Africa and has scored an impress amount of points for the Springboks. Since playing in the Allied Dunbar, he has notched up over 500 points for Saracens

Alain Penaud
Position: Fly Half
Date of Birth: 19 July 1969
Place of Birth: Juillac, France
Height: 6' 0"
Weight: 14st

Alain joins Saracens from European Cup Winners Brive, a club he has spent some eight years with. He has over thirty caps for France and is the noted for his flair and decision making. A good runner and quick thinker, he gets his fair share of tries and has settled into the Saracens squad, where he is a key member and firm crowd favourite.

SECTION 4 – ALLIED DUNBAR PREMIERSHIP

Francois Pienaar
Position: Flanker
Date of Birth: 02 January 1967
Place of Birth: Vereeniging, South Africa
Height: 6' 4"
Weight: 17st

Francois was educated at Patriot School, Witbank in South Africa and played provincial rugby for Transvaal. He made his International debut in 1993 against France and has won 29 caps, culminating in World Cup glory against the All Blacks in 1995.

Francois is now Player/Coach at Saracens in their new home at Vicarage Road, Watford.

Brendan Reidy
Position: Prop
Date of Birth: 13 September 1970
Place of Birth: Apia, Western Samoa
Height: 6' 1"
Weight: 17st

The Western Samoan international made a big impression in England despite only signing late in the 1997/98 season. In his first three league games he showed he could ruck, maul and scrummage effectively and often helped produce good balls for the backs to use. His versatility had been tested and he has settled into the side although instead of playing at his usual position of prop, Brendan entered the fray as the hooker. To go with his other credentials, he's also a fairly fast runner, as some opposition players will testify.

Paul Wallace
Position: Prop
Date of Birth: 30 December 1971
Place of Birth: Cork
Height: 6' 0"
Weight: 16st 12lbs

Paul Wallace was left out of the original Lions Tour party to South Africa but due to his performances throughout the season which on many occasions turned the game in Saracens favour, he was deservedly, selected because of a back injury to Peter Clohessy.

The main attributes of his play are that he is one of the hardest and best tacklers in the league and if Wallace keeps up the form that he has shown over the past two seasons, he should add many more Ireland caps to the fifty since his debut in the 1995 World Cup against Japan.

Richard Wallace
Position: Wing
Date of Birth: 16 January 1968
Place of Birth: Cork
Height: 6' 0"
Weight: 14st

The Irish winger has graced many games around the world with his mesmerising skills and has played twenty-five times for his country and has a Lions Tour under his belt. He is a highly charged and very talented Winger with a full range of skills including side-steps, body swerves, dummy passes, unusual running angles, great pace and trickery. He has scored well over a hundred points in his English league career and is very well respected among fellow professionals.

SECTION 4 – ALLIED DUNBAR PREMIERSHIP

Wasps FC

Ground
Loftus Road Stadium
South Africa Road
Shepherds Bush
London
W12 7PA
Stadium Capacity: 19,000 (seated)

Colours
Shirts: Black, White collar
Shorts: Black
Change Shirts: White, narrow Gold & Black hoops
Shorts: Black

History
Founded: 1867
Number of International Players: 39
Total number of individual caps: 314
First capped player: Pat Sykes, England v France in Paris, 29 March 1948.
Most capped player: (61) Rob Andrew (England 56, Lions 5) (1987-95). Andrew made his first 9 international appearances as a Nottingham player, 5 other caps whilst with Toulouse and also made one replacement appearance as a Newcastle player.
Most tries in tests: 6 in 15 tests by Ted Woodward (1952-56).
Most points in tests: 321 in 61 tests by Rob Andrew (England 310, Lions 11) (1987-95). Andrew scored 86 points whilst a Nottingham player.

Prominent Players
Lawrence Dallaglio

Position: Flanker
Date of Birth: 10 August 1972
Place of Birth: Shepherds Bush
Height: 6' 4"
Weight: 15st 7lbs

Lawrence Dallaglio took over as captain of Wasps when Rob Andrew left in October 1995. He soon established his credentials by leading the club to the first professional English league title the following season. He was a surprise choice for 1994 England tour to South Africa, but established himself on the world game with his performances as part of the victorious 1997 British Lions' tour of South Africa. Has represented England at every level and on his day is one of the world's best back-row players.

His decision to step down as Wasps skipper proved crucial as he regained his form and his England captaincy, the pinnacle of which saw Dallaglio lead England to a shock win over World Champions South Africa. That was the high point, now for the low point – a very public drugs scandal. The extraordinary *News of the World* spread on Lawrence Dallaglio sent shock-waves through the Wasps club, his family and the entire game. He resigned as England captain and didn't tour Australia. During his press conference he stated that he had been foolish and naive to lie about his lifestyle and deeply regretted hurting his family and damaging the reputation of the game, his fellow players, the RFU and his club. Outlining the reasons why this situation had arisen, he said that he was approached by executives purporting to set up a sponsorship deal to promote Gillette's range of shaving products worth £500,000. Additionally he was to front an inner-city programme to help young children. During the course of these negotiations he seems to have been side-tracked into a conversation about drugs. It appears that he was lured by the sham executives talk of drug culture into revealing a teenage dabbling with drugs before embellishing the truth by bragging and lying to string the executives along.

Questioned about his England career, he said that it was out of his hands now. He has the support of his colleagues. The England team would not be helped by the distraction caused by his presence so he resigned. Lawrence could not comment on the motives behind the entrapment but categorically denied that drugs had been used by himself or by anyone on the Lions

SECTION 4 – ALLIED DUNBAR PREMIERSHIP

Will Green
Position: Prop
Date of Birth: 25 October 1973
Place of Birth: Littlehampton
Height: 5' 11"
Weight: 17st 4lbs

Will Green was one of the stars of the Saracens last two league campaigns and made his England test debut against Australia in the pre-Christmas internationals, but had to wait for the summer tour of the Southern Hemisphere to make his second test appearance coming on as a substitute against New Zealand A series of solid performances at tight-head on that tour has established him as a regular member of the England squad. He has represented England at many levels U18, U21, England A and full, but after joining Wasps in February 1992, from the Villagers club, he has improved 100% season upon season.

Rob Henderson
Position: Centre
Date of Birth: 27 October 1972
Place of Birth: Dover
Height: 6' 1"
Weight: 15st 4lbs

Rob Henderson is a physical Irish international centre who joined Wasps midway through the 1996/97 season from London Irish, and played in big part in the league run-in.

In the 1997/98 season he was set back through a string of injuries and although he was arguably Ireland's best back-line player in their Five Nations Campaign he lost his place in the Ireland team for the test against South Africa in the summer. However, he has since reclaimed his place in the International reckoning and it is generally excepted that he is one of the best tacklers in the Premiership.

Alex King
Position: Fly Half
Date of Birth: 17 January 1975
Place of Birth: Brighton
Height: 6' 0"
Weight: 13st 4lbs

One of the brightest talents in the English game, Alex joined Wasps at the start of the 1996/97 season having turned out for Rosslyn Park and Bristol University and played a major part in bringing to league championship to Loftus Road. A series of injuries robbed him of chances for both club and country in the following season and by the time he returned to the Wasps line-up the team teetering on the edge of the relegation zone.

He did regain enough form to play in the Tetley's Bitter Cup Final and was selected for the England tour of New Zealand, Australia and South Africa in the summer but was still short of match fitness and England's poor form was reflected on Alex whose play rapidly deteriorated and he was sent home early. Despite this and the Wasps impressive squad members who are pushing for the Fly half spot, Alex established himself as Wasps first choice number ten and has even managed to force his way back into the England set-up catching the eye as a substitute in the win over South Africa late last year.

SECTION 4 – ALLIED DUNBAR PREMIERSHIP

Kenny Logan
Position: Wing
Date of Birth: 03 April 1972
Place of Birth: Stirling
Height: 6' 1"
Weight: 14st 8lbs

Logan is a very fast and alert Scottish international winger who joined Wasps from Stirling Castle in the 1996/97 season to make an amazing 5-try Wasps debut against Orrell. However, the following season was one Kenny would rather forget. Whilst he wasn't the only player at the club to struggle, his fall from grace was arguably the most dramatic. Eight tries in his first five games (seven in the Heineken Cup) signalled a great season for the twenty-six-year-old Scotland international, but this was a false dawn as a series of mishaps saw him fade in the new year.

First he lost his Scotland place after a heavy defeat at Murrayfield in which he was made a scapegoat for some poor Scottish defence, soon afterwards he lost his Wasps place as the club teetered on the brink of the relegation zone. If things weren't bad enough he then picked up a nagging shoulder injury which forced him to miss the Tetley's Bitter Cup Final and worse ruled him out of Scotland's summer tour of Fiji and Australia. Now fully fit Kenny has regained his form and last season was one of the star performers of the side.

Andy Reed
Position: Lock/Second Row
Date of Birth: 4 May 1969
Place of Birth: St Austell, Cornwall
Height: 6' 7"
Weight: 17st 10lbs

Andy Reed in a very experienced forward who came to Wasps at the start of the 1996/97 season from Bath. He was capped by Scotland in 1993 while at bath and he made the British Lions squad that same year and captained Scotland on their tour of Argentina in 1994. He has over twenty full International test caps for the Scots and Lions', but over the past two seasons has struggled sometimes to keep his place in a very competitive Wasps line-up.

Simon Shaw
Position: Lock
Date of Birth: 01 September 1973
Place of Birth: Nairobi, Kenya
Height: 6' 9"
Weight: 19st

After impressing at his previous clubs of Cranleigh, Pirates (New Zealand) and Bristol, Simon Shaw joined Wasps in September 1997. The 'Gentle Giant" Simon is one of the best lock-forwards in the Premiership having represented England at every level and having been a member of the successful Lions tour to South Africa.

He started the 1997/98 season as an England regular but injury and Wasps indifferent form cost him his England place and even though he fought back to make the England squad for the summer tour of the Southern Hemisphere bad luck struck as he was forced to withdraw with a long standing back injury. Now back to fitness he aims to regain his place in time for the World Cup.

SECTION 4 – ALLIED DUNBAR PREMIERSHIP

Mark Weedon
Position: Lock
Date of Birth: 31 July 1968
Place of Birth: Tauranga, New Zealand
Height: 6' 6"
Weight: 17st

Mark Weedon took over the captaincy from Lawrence Dallaglio in September 1998 and has a very impressive Rugby CV. His former clubs include Ponsonby (Auckland Club Champions), Katikati, Western Suburbs, Massey (North Harbour Club Champions) and Blagnac (France) before joining Wasps. Mark represented New Zealand Secondary Schools in 1986 and was plucked from the Katikati College 1st XV to earn his first class debut for Bay of Plenty. His impressive debut year earned him two early honours. He was named by the New Zealand Rugby Almanac as one of the five promising players for 1986. In recognition of an awesome debut year, he gained selection to tour the United Kingdom with the New Zealand Barbarians in 1987. The core of this team formed the 1987 World Cup winning All Black side and included up-and-coming youngsters such as Va'aiga Tuigamala, Michael Jones and Craig Innes. Mark played two seasons for Bay of Plenty before moving to Auckland to play for the prestigious Ponsonby club, helping them win the Auckland Gallaher Shield in his first year with them.

With a couple of club championships under his belt, he travelled to France to represent Blagnac in 1989 and 1990. After a stint for the Western Suburbs club in Wellington and games for Wellington B he moved to the Massey club in the North Harbour province, repeating his first year performance with Ponsonby by helping Massey win the North Harbour club championship in his first year with them.

It was then that he began to break into the All-blacks scene and a switch to Wasps in 1997 positioned him to develop a solid foundation for the Wasps forward pack and transfer his southern hemisphere knowledge of how to play the new style of rugby where highly developed basic skills of ball winning, retention and handling form a solid platform from which to play the exciting, attacking and free-flowing modern game.

West Hartlepool
Ground
Victoria Park
Clarence Road
Hartlepool
TS24 8BZ
Stadium Capacity: 7,500
Colours
Shirts: Blue, Red and White
Shorts: Blue and White
Change Shirts: Green, Red and White
Shorts: Green and White
History
Founded: 1881
Number of International Players: 7
Total number of individual caps: 33
First capped player: Sam Morfitt, England v Wales at Birkenhead, 6 Jan 1894.
Most capped player: (13) Rob Wainwright (Scotland) (1995-1996). Wainwright played in his first 7 tests as an Edinburgh Academicals player, and has also appeared in his latest 8 tests whilst with Watsonians.
Most tries in tests: 3 in 6 tests by Sam Morfitt (1894-96). Most points in tests: 9 in 6 tests by Sam Morfitt (1894-96).

Prominent Players
Mike Brewer
Position: 8/Flanker
Date of Birth: 6 November 1964
Place of Birth: Pukekohe, New Zealand
Height: 6' 4"
Weight: 16st 3lbs

In an International Test career making over thirty appearances for New Zealand, Mike Brewer is the West Hartlepool main-stay. Apart from his vast experience, his obvious skills and talent bring some quality to a side who were destined to struggle in the Allied Dunbar Premiership. His strong running and link play is always clever and his eye for a try has not evaded him.

SECTION 4 – ALLIED DUNBAR PREMIERSHIP

Mark Giacheri
Position: Flanker
Date of Birth: 1 February 1969
Place of Birth: Sydney, Australia
Height: 6' 8"
Weight: 17st 11lbs

This Australian born Italian has performed wonders in the back row for West Hartlepool, like Mike Brewer, he is a kingpin in the set-up and brings experience and a cool head to the battle. He has over thirty full International test caps for Italy and has become a Victoria Park crowd favourite. He is a tough competitor and like to get forward.

Toby Handley
Position: Scrum Half
Date of Birth: 14 April 1976
Place of Birth: Catterick
Height: 5ft 9in
Weight: 12st 3lbs

Catterick born Toby Handley is a young Scrum half with plenty of promise. He started his rugby career as a youngster with Durham City before tasting the high life with the South African team of Harlequins. This promising students representative honours: include appearances for County Colts & U21's, but he is yet to make and impact at International level. He is a fast and agile player with much of potential.

Patrick Seymour
Position: Prop
Date of Birth: 18 July 1978
Place of Birth: Northallerton
Height: 6ft
Weight: 17st 7lbs

This hard-hitting young prop has represented Middlesbrough and Harrogate before joining the staff at the Victoria Ground. He has a good level of representative honours including appearances for Durham County Under-15's to 18's as captain, Yorkshire Colts and Under-21's and England Colts and under 21's. His first season in West Hartlepool colours was impressive and Patrick is being tipped as a future full England international.

Allied Dunbar Division 1 clubs

Blackheath FC

Ground
The Rectory Field
Charlton Road
Blackheath
London
SE3 8SR
Stadium Capacity: 3,500

Colours
Shirts: Black & Red hoops with thin Cambridge Blue line separating
Shorts: Black
Change Shirts: Cambridge Blue with thick Black and thin Red hoops
Shorts: Black

History
Founded: 1858
Number of international players: 131
Total number of individual caps: 473
First capped player: Frederic Stokes, Charles Sherrard, Benjamin Burns and Charles Crompton all for England v Scotland in Edinburgh, 27 March 1871 (the first ever test match).
Most capped player: (20): Cherry Pillman (England 18, Lions 2) (1910-14)
Most tries in tests: 10 in 16 tests by Cyril Lowe (1920-23). Lowe made his first 9 test appearances as a Cambridge University player and scored 8 tries.
Most points in tests: 40 in 12 tests by Lennard Stokes (1875-81).

SECTION 4 – ALLIED DUNBAR PREMIERSHIP

Bristol FC

Ground
Memorial Ground
Filton Avenue
Horfield
Bristol
BS7 0AQ
Stadium Capacity: 10,000

Colours
Shirts: Blue & White hoops
Shorts: Blue
Change Shirts: Blue & Amber quarters
Shorts: Blue

History
Founded: 1888
Number of international players: 52
Total number of individual caps: 361
First capped player: John Jarman, Great Britain v Australia at Sydney, 24 June 1899.
Most capped player: (48) John Pullin (England 41, British Lions 7) (1966 to 1976).
Most tries in tests: 3 in 3 tests by Jack Spoors (Lions 1910), 3 in 8 tests by Donald Burland (1931-33), 3 in 16 tests by Leonard Corbett (1921-27).
Most points in tests: 102 in 16 tests by Jon Webb (1987-89). Webb also scored 194 points in seventeen tests as a Bath player.

Coventry RFC

Ground

Barkers Butts Lane
Coundon
Coventry
CV6 1DU

Stadium Capacity: 7,500

Colours

Shirts: Dark Blue and White stripes
Shorts: Dark Blue
Change Shirts: Red and White stripes
Shorts: White

History

Founded: 1874

Number of international players: 43

Total number of individual caps: 303

First capped player: W Judkins, Great Britain v Australia at Brisbane, 22 July 1899.

Most capped player: (39): David Duckham (England 36, Lions 3)(1969-76)

Most tries in tests: 10 in 39 tests by David Duckham (1969-76)

Most points in tests: 36 in 39 tests by David Duckham (1969-76)

SECTION 4 – ALLIED DUNBAR PREMIERSHIP

Exeter RFC

Ground
The County Ground
Church Road
St Thomas
Exeter
Devon
EX2 9BQ
Stadium Capacity: 6,000

Colours
Shirts: Black, White collar
Shorts: Black
Change Shirts: White, thin black hoop
Shorts: Black

History
Founded: 1872
Number of international players: 11
Total Number of individual caps: 33
First capped player: Richard Kindersley, England v Scotland at Blackheath, 1 March 1884
Most capped player: 12 by Thomas Kelly (1906-08)
Most tries in tests: 2 in 2 tests by Richard Kindersley (1884-85)
Most points in tests: 2 in 2 tests by Richard Kindersley (1884-85).
Kindersley made his test debut in 1882 as an Oxford University player

Fylde FC

Ground Woodlands Memorial Ground
Blackpool Road, Ansdell
Lytham St Annes
Lancashire FY8 1AB
Stadium Capacity: 5,450

Colours
Shirts: Claret, Gold & White hoops
Shorts: White
Change Shirts: Claret
Shorts: White

History
Founded: 1919
Number of international players: 4
Total number of individual caps: 71
First capped player: Malcolm Phillips, England v Wales at Cardiff, 21 Jan 1961. Phillips made his first dozen test appearances as an Oxford University player and scored one try.
Most capped player:(41) Bill Beaumont (England 34, Lions 7) (1975-82)
Most tries in tests: 4 in 13 tests by Malcolm Phillips (1961-64).
Most points in tests: 12 in 13 tests by Malcolm Phillips (1961-64).

SECTION 4 – ALLIED DUNBAR PREMIERSHIP

Leeds Tykes RFC
Ground
Headingley Stadium
St Michael's Lane
Headingley
LS6 3BR
Stadium Capacity: 22,000
Colours
Shirts: Blue with Gold and White stripes
Shorts: Blue
Change Shirts: White with Blue and Gold stripes
Shorts: Blue
History
Founded: 1877 Headingley, 1923 Roundhay, 1992 Leeds
Number of international players: 28 (since WW1)
Total number of individual caps: 186
First capped player: Aarvold (1928) for England.
Most capped player: Ian McGeeghan (32 for Scotland).

London Welsh RFC
Ground
Old Deer Park
Kew Road, Richmond
Surrey
TW9 2AZ
Stadium Capacity: 5,850
Colours
Shirts: Red (Black stripe)
Shorts: Black
Change Shirts: Black (Red stripe)
Shorts: Black
History
Founded: 1885
First capped player: A J Gould 1885-86
Most capped player: JPR Williams (55)
Number of capped players: 196 plus 18 British Lions (world record 7 on tour to New Zealand 1971).

Moseley RFC

Ground
The Reddings
Reddings Road
Moseley
B13 8LW
Stadium Capacity: 5,000

Colours
Shirts: Red & Black
Shorts: Black
Change Shirts: Light Grey / Navy Hoops
Shorts: Black

History
Founded: 1873
Number of international players: 27
Total number of individual caps: 171
First capped player: John Rogers, England v Wales at Dewsbury, 15 February 1890.
Most capped player: (15) Colin McFadyean (England 11, Lions 4) 1966-68).
Most tries in tests: (5): Colin McFadyean (4 in 11 tests for England, 1 in 4 tests for Lions)(1966-68).
Most points in tests:(36): Fred Byrne (24 in 13 tests for England, 12 in 4 tests for Lions) (1894-1899).

SECTION 4 – ALLIED DUNBAR PREMIERSHIP

Orrell FC
Ground
Edge Hall Road
Orrell
Wigan
WN5 8TL
Stadium Capacity: 6,500
Colours
Shirts: Amber with wide Black horizontal stripe
Shorts: Black
Change Shirts: Amber, Black and Red narrow horizontal stripes
Shorts: Black
History
Founded: 1927
Number of international players: 8
Total number of individual caps: 78
First capped player: Frank Anderson, England v New Zealand at Twickenham, 6 Jan 1973.
Most capped player:(32): John Carleton (England 26, Lions 6)(1979-84).
Most tries in tests: 7 in 32 tests by John Carleton (1979-84).
Most points in tests: 28 in 32 tests by John Carleton (1979-84).

Rotherham RUFC
Ground
Clifton Lane Sports Ground
Badsley Moor Lane
Rotherham
South Yorkshire
S65 2AA
Stadium Capacity: 5,000
Colours
Shirts: Burgundy, Sky Blue/Navy Blue stripes
Shorts: Black
Change Strip: None
History
Founded: 1923
Number of International Players: N/A

Rugby RFC

Ground
Webb Ellis Road
Rugby
CV22 7AU
Stadium Capacity: 3,912
Colours
Shirts: White with Red Lion
Shorts: Blue
Change Shirts: Red with White edging
Shorts: Blue
History
Founded: 1873
Number of international players: 16
First capped player: SJ Purdy, (England v Scotland) (1962)
Most capped player: 20 by GS Conway (England – 1920-27)

Wakefield RFC

Ground
College Grove
Eastmoor Road
Wakefield WF1 3RR
Stadium Capacity: 3,000
Colours
Shirts: Black & Gold quarters
Shorts: Black
Change Shirts: Red with Black collar
Shorts: Black
History
Founded: 1901
Number of international players: 8
Total number of individual caps: 30
First capped player: N/A
Most capped player: (15) Mike Harrison (1985-88).
Most tries in tests: 8 in 15 tests by Mike Harrison (1985-88).
Most points in tests: 32 in 15 by Mike Harrison (1985-88).

SECTION 4 - ALLIED DUNBAR PREMIERSHIP

Waterloo Rugby
Ground:
St Anthony's Road
Blundell Sands
Liverpool
L23 8TW
Stadium Capacity: 9,000
Colours
Shirts: Red, White, Myrtle hoops
Shorts: Myrtle
Change Shirts: Blue, White quarters
Shorts: Black
History
Founded: 1882
Number of international players: 25
Total number of individual caps: 139
First capped player: Samuel McQueen, Scotland v France at Inverleith, 20 Jan 1923.
Most capped player: (21) Joe Periton (1925-30)
Most tries in tests: (6) Joe Periton (1925-30)
Most points in tests: (18) Joe Periton (1925-30)

Worcester RFC
Ground
Sixways
Pershore Lane
Hindlip
Worcester
WR3 8ZE
Stadium Capacity: 4,200
/Colours
Shirts: Old Gold with Navy Blue banded stripes
Shorts: Navy
Change Shirts: Navy with Red and Old Gold banded stripes
Shorts: Navy
History
Founded: 1871

SECTION 5 – FACTS AND FEATS

Facts and Feats – Odds and Sods

The following section gives details of many things. Club Rugby Union competitions from around the world, a round-up of the World Cup statistics, details on important international competitions and other facts from the world of rugby, such as the Olympic games.

First International Fixtures
The following list gives a 'timeline' indication of the first recorded International fixtures in the development of World Rugby union.

1871	Scotland Vs England
1875	England Vs Ireland
1881	England Vs Wales
1883	Ireland Vs Scotland,
	Scotland Vs Wales
1884	Ireland Vs Wales
1891	British Isles (Lions) Vs South Africa
1903	Australia Vs New Zealand
1904	British Isles (Lions) Vs New Zealand
1905	England Vs New Zealand
	Ireland Vs New Zealand
	Wales Vs New Zealand
	Scotland Vs New Zealand
1906	England Vs South Africa
	Ireland Vs South Africa
	Wales Vs South Africa
	Scotland Vs South Africa
	France Vs New Zealand
1908	Wales Vs Australia
1909	England Vs Australia
	Ireland Vs France
1910	England Vs France
	Wales Vs France

....	Scotland Vs France
1912	United States Vs Australia
1913	New Zealand Vs United States
....	France Vs South Africa
1920	France Vs United States
1921	New Zealand Vs South Africa
1924	France Vs Romania
1927	France Vs Germany
1930	British Isles (Lions) Vs Australia
1933	South Africa Vs Australia
1937	France Vs Italy
1947	Scotland Vs Australia
....	Ireland Vs Australia
1948	France Vs Australia
1949	France Vs Argentina
1952	Australia Vs Fiji
1956	France Vs Czechoslovakia
1964	France Vs Fiji
1973	Australia Vs Tonga
....	France Vs Japan
1975	Australia Vs Japan
1979	Australia Vs Argentina
1981	Scotland Vs Romania
....	Romania Vs New Zealand
....	South Africa Vs United States
....	Argentina Vs England
1983	Australia Vs Italy
....	Romania Vs Wales
1985	Argentina Vs New Zealand
....	Australia Vs Canada
....	Wales Vs Fiji
....	England Vs Romania
1986	Wales Vs Tonga
....	Wales Vs Western Samoa
....	Ireland Vs Romania
1987	Australia Vs Korea
....	Scotland Vs Zimbabwe
....	New Zealand Vs Italy
....	Ireland Vs Tonga

SECTION 5 – FACTS AND FEATS

	New Zealand Vs Fiji
	France Vs Zimbabwe
	England Vs United States
	Wales Vs Canada
	Ireland Vs Canada
	Wales Vs United States
	England Vs Japan
1988	Ireland Vs Western Samoa
	Ireland Vs Italy
	Fiji Vs England
1989	Scotland Vs Fiji
1990	Ireland Vs Argentina
	Wales Vs Namibia
	Scotland Vs Argentina
1991	Ireland Vs Namibia
	France Vs Canada
	Australia Vs Western Samoa
	New Zealand Vs Canada
	Wales Vs Argentina
	Scotland Vs Japan
	England Vs Italy
	Ireland Vs Japan
	Ireland Vs Zimbabwe
	Scotland Vs Western Samoa
1992	England Vs Canada
1993	New Zealand Vs Western Samoa
1995	New Zealand Vs Japan

Scores Evolution in Rugby Union

Below is a timeline table of the worth of a score in rugby. Notice that a Try started off life as being worth only 1 point, but it is now worth five! Whereas, a drop goal started off at 3 points, was raised to 4 and is now worth only 3 again.

Year	1891	1892-93	1894-95	1896-1947	1948-71	1972-91	1992-96
Try	1 pt	2	3	3	3	4	5
Kick	2	3	2	2	2	2	2
Penalties	2	3	3	3	3	3	3
Drop	3	4	4	3	3	3	3

World Cup Records Final tournaments – (1987, 1991, 1995)
Winners of the William Webb Ellis Trophy
20/6/1987: New Zealand (beat France 29-9 in the final, Auckland)
2/11/1991: Australia (beat England 12-6 in the final, London)
24/6/1995: South Africa (beat New Zealand 15-12 in the final, Johannesburg, after 20 minutes extra time)

Country Records
Highest score:
145 New Zealand beat Japan 145-17 (1995, Bloemfontein)

Biggest winning margin:
128 New Zealand beat Japan 145-17 (1995, Bloemfontein)

Most points scored by both teams in a match:
162 New Zealand beat Japan 145-17 (1995)

Most points in a match:
145 New Zealand (1995: Vs Japan)
89 Scotland (1995: Vs Ivory Coast)
74 New Zealand (1987: Vs Fiji)
70 New Zealand (1987: Vs Italy)
70 France (1987: Vs Zimbabwe)

Most tries scored by a country:
103 New Zealand (1987, 1991, 1995 in 18 matches)

Most tries by a team in a tournament:
43 New Zealand (1987: 6 matches)
41 New Zealand (1995: 6 matches)

Most tries in a match:
21 New Zealand (1995: Vs Japan)

Most penalties in a match:
8 Scotland (1995: Vs Tonga)
8 France (1995: Vs Ireland)
6 New Zealand (1987: Vs Scotland)

SECTION 5 – FACTS AND FEATS

6 New Zealand (1987: Vs Argentina)

Most conversions in a tournament:
20 New Zealand (1995: Vs Japan)

Most drop goals in a match:
3 Fiji (1991: Vs Romania)

Individual Records

Most matches:
17 Sean Fitzpatrick (New Zealand: 1987, 1991, 1995)
15 Rory Underwood (England: 1987, 1991, 1995)
15 David Campese (Australia: 12987, 1991, 1995)
15 Michael Lynagh (Australia: 1987, 1991, 1995)

Most points in all world cup matches:
227 Gavin Hastings (Scotland: 1987, 1991, 1995)
195 Michael Lynagh (Australia: 1987, 1991, 1995)
170 Grant Fox (New Zealand, 1987, 1991)
112 Thierry Lacroix (France: 1995)

Most points in a tournament:
126 Grant Fox (New Zealand: 6 matches in 1995)
112 Thierry Lacroix (France: 6 matches in 1995)
104 Gavin Hastings (Scotland: 6 matches in 1995)

Most points in a match:
45 Simon Culhane (1995: New Zealand Vs Japan)
44 Gavin Hastings (1995: Scotland Vs Ivory Coast)
31 Gavin Hastings (1995: Scotland Vs Tonga)
30 Didier Camberabero (1987: France Vs Zimbabwe)
30 Masc Ellis (1995: New Zealand Vs Japan)

Most tries in all world cup matches:
11 Rory Underwood (England: 1987, 1991, 1995)
10 David Campese (Australia: 1987, 1991, 1995)
9 Gavin Hastings (Scotland: 1987, 1991, 1995)
7 John Kirwan (New Zealand: 1987, 1991)

7 Marc Ellis (New Zealand: 1995)
7 Jonah Lomu (New Zealand: 1995)

Most tries in a tournament:
7 Marc Ellis (New Zealand, 1995)
7 Jonah Lomu (New Zealand, 1995)
6 Craig Green (New Zealand, 1987)
6 John Kirwan (New Zealand, 1987)
6 David Campese (Australia, 1991)
6 Jean-Baptiste Lafond (France, 1991)

Most tries in a match:
6 Marc Ellis (1995: New Zealand Vs Japan)
4 Ieuan Evans (1987: Wales Vs Canada)
4 Craig Green (1987: New Zealand Vs Fiji)
4 John Gallagher (1987: New Zealand Vs Fiji)
4 Brian Robinson (1991: Ireland Vs Zimbabwe)
4 Gavin Hastings (1995: Scotland Vs Ivory Coast)
4 Chester Williams (1995: South Africa Vs Western Samoa)
4 Jonah Lomu (1995: New Zealand Vs England)

Most penalties in world cup matches:
31 Michael Lynagh (Australia: 1987, 1991, 1995)
27 Grant Fox (New Zealand: 1987, 1991)
27 Gavin Hastings (Scotland: 1987, 1991, 1995)

Most penalties in a tournament:
21 Grant Fox (New Zealand, 1987)
16 Ralph Keyes (Ireland, 1991)

Most penalties in a match:
8 Gavin Hastings (1995: Scotland Vs Tonga)
8 Thierry Lacroix (1995: France Vs Ireland)

Most drop goals in all matches:
5 Rob Andrew (England: 1991, 1995)

Most drop goals in a tournament:
3 Jonathan Davies (Wales, 1987)

SECTION 5 – FACTS AND FEATS

3 Joel Stransky (South Africa, 1995)
3 Rob Andrew (England: 1995)
3 Andrew Mehrtens (New Zealand, 1995)

Most drop goals in a match:
2 Jonathan Davies (1987: Wales Vs Ireland)
2 Lizano Arbizu (1991: Argentina Vs Australia)
2 T Rabaka (1991: Fiji Vs Romania)
2 Rob Andrew (1995: England Vs Argentina)
2 Joel Stransky (1995 Final: South Africa Vs New Zealand)

Most conversions in a tournament:
30 Grant Fox (New Zealand, 1987)
20 Michael Lynagh (Australia, 1987)
20 Simon Culhane (New Zealand, 1995)

Most conversions in a tournament:
20 Simon Culhane (1995: New Zealand Vs Japan)

Most points in a match:
50 Ashley Billington (1994: Hong Kong Vs Singapore)
34 Jamie McKee (1994: Hong Kong Vs Singapore)

Attendance Records
Spectators at a tournament
1987: 604,500
1991: 1,007,760
1995: 1,100,000
Most spectators at a match
63,000 1995 Final South Africa Vs New Zealand, Ellis Park, Johannesburg
60,208 1991 Final Australia Vs England, Twickenham, London
Least spectators at a match
5,000 1991: Canada Vs Fiji, Bayonne, France Qualifying tournament

Team Records
Biggest win and most points:
164-13 Hong Kong Vs Singapore (27/10/1994, Kuala Lumpur)

Most points in a match:
164 Hong Kong beat Singapore 164-13 (27/10/1994), Kuala Lumpur
134 Japan beat Taiwan 134-6 (27/10/1998), Singapore
104 Italy beat Czech Republic 104-9 (18/5/1994), Vianda
102 Wales beat Portugal 102-11 (17/5/1994), Lisbon, Portugal
102 Italy beat Denmark 102-3 (1/11/1997), Brescia

Most tries in a match:
26 Hong Kong Vs Singapore (1994)
20 Japan Vs Taiwan (1998)

Tri Nations Series Records

Biggest victory:
By 39 points: SA 61 Aus 22 (Pretoria: 23/8/97)

Most points in match:
61 – SA beat Aus 61-22)

Most points in a match by losing team:
35 – NZ beat SA 55-35 (9/8/97)

Most points in a season:
159 – New Zealand (1997)

Most tries in a match:
8 – SA beat Aus 61-22 (23/8/97)

Most tries in a match by a losing team:
5 – NZ beat SA 55-35 (9/8/97)

Most tries in a season:
18 – South Africa (1997)

Most victories:
8 – New Zealand; 6: South Africa; 4: Australia

Most defeats:
8 – Australia; 6: South Africa; 4: New Zealand

SECTION 5 – FACTS AND FEATS

Individual Series Records

Most points in a match:
26 – Jannie de Beer (SA, beat Aus 61-22; 23/8/97)

Most points in a season:
84 – Carlos Spencer (NZ, 1997)

Most tries in a match:
2 – Ben Tune (Aus, Vs SA: 2/8/97)
2 – Christian Cullen (NZ, Vs SA; 9/8/97)
2 – Stephen Larkham (Aus, Vs NZ; 16/8/97)
2 – Percy Montgomery (SA, Vs Aus; 23/8/97)
2 – Matthew Burke (Aus, Vs NZ; 11/7/98)

Most tries in a season:
4 – Christian Cullen (NZ)

Most points in the competition:
94 – Andrew Mehrtens (NZ)
90 – Matthew Burke (Aus)

Most tries in the competition:
6 – Christian Cullen (NZ)

Tri Nation Results

Tri Nations Series – 1996

06/07/96	Wellington	New Zealand (43)	Australia (6)
13/07/96	Sydney	Australia (21)	South Africa (16)
20/07/96	Christchurch	New Zealand (15)	South Africa (11)
27/07/96	Brisbane	Australia (25)	New Zealand (32)
03/08/96	Bloemfontein	South Africa (25)	Australia (19)
10/08/96	Cape Town	New Zealand (29)	South Africa (18)

Tri Nations Series – 1997

19/07/97	Johannesburg	New Zealand (35)	South Africa (32)
26/07/97	Melbourne	New Zealand (33)	Australia (18)
02/08/97	Brisbane	Australia (32)	South Africa (20)

09/08/97	Auckland	New Zealand (55)	South Africa (35)
16/08/97	Dunedin	New Zealand (36)	Australia (24)
23/08/97	Pretoria	South Africa (61)	Australia (22)

Tri Nations Series – 1998
11/07/98	Melbourne	Australia (24)	New Zealand (16)
18/07/98	Perth	South Africa (14)	Australia (13)
25/07/98	Wellington	South Africa (13)	New Zealand (3)
01/08/98	Christchurch	Australia (27)	New Zealand (23)
15/08/98	Durban	South Africa (24)	New Zealand (23)
22/08/98	Johannesburg	South Africa (29)	Australia (15)

Tri Nations Series – 1999
Fixtures
10/07/99	Dunedin	New Zealand V South Africa
17/07/99	Brisbane	Australia V South Africa
24/07/99	Auckland	New Zealand V Australia
07/08/99	Pretoria	South Africa V New Zealand
14/08/99	Cape Town	South Africa V Australia
28/08/99	Sydney	Australia V New Zealand

Domestic Tournaments
Currie Cup
First held in 1889, the Currie Cup is South Africa's Inter-provincial tournament.

Here are the winners since 1939:

Year	Winners
1939	Golden Lions
1946	Blue Bulls
1947	Western Province
1950	Golden Lions
1952	Golden Lions
1954	Western Province
1956	Blue Bulls
1968	Blue Bulls
1969	Blue Bulls
1970	Griqualand West
1971	Golden Lions

SECTION 5 – FACTS AND FEATS

Year	Winner
1972	Golden Lions
1973	Blue Bulls
1974	Blue Bulls
1975	Blue Bulls
1976	Free State
1977	Blue Bulls
1978	Blue Bulls
1979	Western Province
1980	Blue Bulls
1981	Blue Bulls
1982	Western Province
1983	Western Province
1984	Western Province
1985	Western Province
1986	Western Province
1987	Blue Bulls
1988	Blue Bulls
1989	Blue Bulls & Western Province
1990	Natal
1991	Blue Bulls
1992	Natal
1993	Golden Lions
1994	Golden Lions
1995	Natal
1996	Natal
1997	Western Province
1998	Blue Bulls

Vodacom Cup Finals

Date	Venue	Winner	Runner-up
24/5/1996	Free State Stadium	Free State 46	Border 34
14/5/1997	Newlands, Cape Town	Western Province 36	Boland 25
30/5/1998	Absa Park, Kimberley	Griqualand West 57	Golden Lions 0
29/5/1999	Ellis Park, Johannesburg	Lions 73	Griqualand West 7

Final Top Try Scorers Vodacom Cup

Number of tries	Players Name and Province
12	Dean Hall (Lions)
	Roger Smith (Griqualand West)
11	Jaco Booysen (Lions)
9	Hennie le Roux (Lions)
8	Luther Bakkes (Griqualand West)
	Francois Grootboom (Gauteng Falcons)
	Gavin Passens (Northern Free State Griffons)
	Ashwell Rafferty (Free State Cheetahs)
7	Peet Arnold (Blue Bulls)
	Kallie Benadie (Mpumalangs Pumas)
	Kobus Engelbrecht (Lions)
	Johan Roets (Blue Bulls)
	Chaka Willemse (Mpumalanga Pumas)
6	Jan Ackermann (Boland Cavaliers)
	Thinus Delport (Lions)
	Friedrich Lombard (FS Cheetahs)
	Coenie Malherbe (Boland Cavaliers)
	Walter Minnaar (Lions)
	Torros Pretorius (Mpumalanga Pumas)
	Hakkies Swart (Mpumalanga Pumas)
	Wickus Venter (Lions)
5	Grant Bartle (Mpumalanga Pumas)
	Tom Cameron (Griqualand West)
	Johan de Kock (Northern Free State Griffons)
	Dawie du Toit (Gauteng Falcons)
	Dale Heidtmann (Eastern Province Elephants)
	Grant Henderson (KZN Wildebeest)
	Wayne Julies (Boland Cavaliers)
	Edrich Lubbe (Griqualand West)
	Rickus Lubbe (SWD Eagles)
	Mac Masina (Lions)
	Kaya Molatana (Border Bulldogs)
	Jacob Muchepa (Mpumalanga Pumas)
	Riaan Olckers (Griquland West)
	Len van Riet (Gauteng Falcons)

SECTION 5 – FACTS AND FEATS

New Zealand League
The national league championships in new Zealand were inaugurated in 1976. Here is a list of all the winners.

1976	Bay of Plenty
1977	Canterbury
1978	Wellington
1979	Counties
1980	Manawatu
1981	Wellington
1982	Auckland
1983	Canterbury
1984	Auckland
1985	Auckland
1986	Wellington
1987	Auckland
1988	Auckland
1989	Auckland
1990	Auckland
1991	Otago
1992	Waikato
1993	Auckland
1994	Auckland
1995	Auckland

From 1996, the league has been known as the Super 12 with teams from New Zealand and Australia taking part. Here are the winners

1996	Auckland
1997	Auckland
1998	Canterbury

French Championship
The country's premier Rugby Union club competition has been running since 1892. Here is a list of the winners since 1980.

1980	AS Beziers
1981	AS Beziers
1982	SU Agen
1983	AS Beziers
1984	AS Beziers
1985	Toulouse

1986	Toulouse
1987	RC Toulon
1988	SU Agen
1989	Toulouse
1990	Racing club de France
1991	CA Begles
1992	RC Toulon
1993	Caskes Olympique
1994	Toulouse
1995	Toulouse
1996	Toulouse
1997	Toulouse

English League

Known as the Courage League until the 1997/98 season, this competition is now the Allied Dunbar Premiership. Here is a list of winners since it's inception.

1985/86	Gloucester
1986/87	Bath
1987/88	Leicester
1988/89	Bath
1989/90	Wasps
1990/91	Bath
1991/92	Bath
1992/93	Bath
1993/94	Bath
1994/95	Leicester
1995/96	Bath
1996/97	Wasps
1997/98	Newcastle
1998/99	Leicester

Welsh League

This competition was introduced in the 1990/91 season. Here is a list of the champions from each year.

1990/91	Neath
1991/92	Swansea
1992/93	Llanelli
1993/94	Swansea

SECTION 5 – FACTS AND FEATS

1994/95	Cardiff
1995/96	Neath
1996/97	Pontypridd

Scottish League
Here is a list of the Scottish League champions since the 1973/74 season.

1973/74	Hawick
1974/75	Hawick
1975/76	Hawick
1977/78	Hawick
1978/79	Heriots Former Pupils
1979/80	Gala
1980/81	Gala
1981/82	Hawick
1982/83	Gala
1983/84	Hawick
1984/85	Hawick
1985/86	Hawick
1986/87	Hawick
1987/88	Kelso
1988/89	Kelso
1989/90	Melrose
1990/91	Boroughmuir
1991/92	Melrose
1992/93	Melrose
1993/94	Melrose
1994/95	Stirling County
1995/96	Melrose
1996/97	Melrose

The Irish Rugby Football Union
The IRFU has direct control over just one competition. This is the AIB All Ireland League Competition for senior clubs.

The competition was inaugurated in season 1990/1991 and expanded to a four division competition for season 1993/94. A feature of the All Ireland League has been its continued development for the betterment of Irish rugby. In 1995/96 the provincial leagues acted as qualifiers for the AIL and the respective winners, Suttonians (Leinster), Ballynahinch (Ulster), Richmond (Munster) and Creggs (Connacht) gained promotion to Division 4 of the League. The following year, the four provincial winners engaged in a round robin qualifying tournament with the overall winners gaining automatic entry to AIL 4. The round robin runner-up was then pitted against the second last placed side in Division 4 with the winner of that play-off securing a place in the All Ireland League Last year (1997/98) saw the introduction of a knockout phase at the end of the league campaign to decide the eventual winner and that system remained in place for the season just ended.

The four division format will be retained for this coming season (1999/2000) but in addition it has been decided to apply the system of match points and bonus points used so successfully in the 1998/99 Guinness Interprovincial Championship. 4 points for a win, 2 for a draw, 1 bonus point for scoring 4 or more tries and 1 bonus point if beaten by 7 points or less. The season 2000/20001 will see further change with a three division sixteen club competition, each division divided into two sections of equal merit with clubs playing each other home and away. The top two clubs in each section will qualify for semi-finals, in which the winner of one section will play the runner-up of the other. This applies in all three divisions with finals at Lansdowne Road.

The Guinness Interprovincial Championship begins in 1999 on the week-end of August 6th with defending champions Munster at home to Leinster. European Cup holders, Ulster, who finished runner-up in last year's competition, travel to Galway for their opening game against Connacht. The Guinness Interprovincial Championship which was played on a home and away basis for the first time, ended on a high note with three provinces in contention for the title going into the last round of games. The record crowds who turned up at Donnybrook and Ravenhill were treated to some thrilling rugby with Munster snatching the trophy by virtue of their 25-10 win over defending champions Leinster. Up north Ulster beat Connacht 36-6 and the extra point they gained by scoring four tries gave them a vital bonus point and second place in the final table. The innovative new Super 12 style scoring system which gave bonus points for try scoring and for keeping losses within seven points proved a huge success with an average of four tries being scored in each match.

Epson Cup – Pacific Rim

The fifteen-match, ten-week long 1999 Epson Cup Pacific Rim championship is in its first year. The new tournament stands on the most solid of platforms with three of the six competing teams, Canada, Japan

SECTION 5 – FACTS AND FEATS

and USA, foundation members of the original Pacific Rim competition, launched in 1996 by the three unions and Hong Kong.

With funding from the International Rugby Board of up to £400,000 for each of the next three years, the tournament has been expanded to include the three Pacific Islands, Fiji, Samoa and Tonga. The Islands are recognised as well-established, quality opponents who, until now, had difficulty in securing regular international fixtures outside their own geographic area. Close co-operation between the six countries, working to the tightest of deadlines earlier this year, has provided each of them with a demanding schedule of five tests between 1 May and 3 July 1999.

With the Seiko Epson Corporation, of Tokyo, supporting the event as its first title sponsor, the new tournament has been renamed the Epson Cup Pacific Rim. Hong Kong, with some players unable to meet the IRB's Regulation 7 eligibility requirements, dropped out of contention with Argentina expected in next year (2000) as the seventh contestant.

The Epson Cup becomes the world's third major annual international rugby competition after the Five (Six) Nations, with Italy joining England, France, Ireland, Scotland and Wales in 2000, and SANZAR, involving South Africa, New Zealand and Australia.

Canada, defeated only once in each of the first three years of the original Pacific Rim competition, have three successive championships to their credit. The USA were runners-up in 1996, as were Hong Kong in 1997 and again in 1998.

From here on the competition will be greatly enhanced by the inclusion of the South Pacific trio. Based on results since the 1995 Rugby World Cup, Samoa are rated seventh among the world's top 12 teams with Canada tenth.

The new tournament has come at just the right time providing an ideal testing ground as the six teams look ahead to Rugby World Cup 1999. Canada, Fiji, Japan, Samoa, USA and Tonga have all qualified for this year's Rugby World Cup in Europe.

Four of the six Epson Cup rivals will have a chance to measure up one of their RWC '99 pool challengers. Japan and Samoa are in the Welsh group and play again in Wrexham on 3 October. Canada and Fiji travel to France, as they did in RWC '91, and are paired for the second time this year in Bordeaux, on 9 October. The USA will compete in the Ireland pool, with Tonga heading for England.

Keiji Hirose kicked nine penalties, a conversion and scored a try to help Japan rout Tonga 44-17 on Saturday 8 May 1999 in the Epson Cup

Pacific Rim Rugby Championship at the Prince Chichibu Memorial Rugby Ground in Tokyo. It was the second victory in as many games to start the six-nation tournament for Japan, which has never won more than two games in each of the event's first three years.

Rugby at the Olympic Games

Introduced by Baron Pierre de Coubertin (who refereed the first ever French championship final), rugby was on the Olympic program at Paris in 1900, at London in 1908, Antwerp in 1920, and Paris again in 1924. In 1928 the International Olympic Committee turned down the request to stage rugby at the Amsterdam games. Three factors were believed to be behind this: the IOC wanted more emphasis on individual sports; women's athletics had swollen the number of competitors; and the sport did not receive the backing that it should have from the British entries. Both the Soviet Union in 1980 and South Korea in 1988 made attempts to have rugby readmitted, and it should be pointed out that South Korea came desperately close to achieving their aim.

1900 Paris – Three teams entered - France, Germany and Britain. France won the gold, winning 27-17 against Germany, who were awarded the silver medal. Britain lost 27-8 to France in the only other match, and were awarded the bronze.

1908 London – Two teams entered - Britain, the hosts, and Australia. Just one match was played, a straight final, won by Australia 32-3.

1912 Stockholm – Rugby tournament not held.

1920 Antwerp – Two teams entered – USA and France. The USA caused a shock by winning the only match 8-0 to take the gold medal.

1924 Paris –Three teams entered - France, USA, and Romania. Each country played two games. Both France and USA beat Romania, who were awarded the bronze medal. France won 59-3, scoring 13 tries including four by the fine Staid Francais winger Adolphe Jaureguy. The USA then defeated Romania 39-0. The final was played at the Columbus stadium, Paris on 18 May 1924 and the USA took the gold with a 17-3 victory before 30,000. The Americans, from Stanford University, scored five tries (Farrish (2), Patrick, Rogers and Manelli), with a conversion from Doe. Gallau scored the lone French try. The match finished in uproar, when Gideon Nelson, one of the reserves, was flattened by a walking stick. The American anthem was jeered, and rugby ceased at the Olympics.

Dual gold medallists –Daniel Carroll was a member of the Australian gold medal team in 1908, and won another gold for the USA in 1920.

SECTION 5 – FACTS AND FEATS

Morris Kirksey, gold medallist in the sprint relay and silver medallist in the 100 metres on the track in 1920, was a member of the gold medal rugby team in 1920. Kirksey failed by 18 inches (46cm) to beat Charlie Paddock for the sprint gold.

	Won	Lost	For	Against	Gold	Silver	Bronze
USA	3	0	64	3	2	-	-
France	3	2	116	53	1	2	-
Australia	1	0	32	3	1	-	-
Germany	0	1	17	27	-	1	-
Britain	0	2	11	59	-	1	1
Romania	0	2	3	98	-	-	1

Snippets
The most capped International player
Phillipe Sella of France played 111 tests for France until his retirement from international rugby in December 1995. He made his debut against Romania in 1982 and played his last game for France at the 1995 World Cup in the third place playoff against England. In second place is Serge Blanco (also of France but now retired) who played (I think) 93 tests. Next closest is David Campese with 91 (still playing but out of favour with the Australian selectors).

Most tries in test Rugby
David Campese of Australia scored 63 tries in International test Rugby, making him the greatest trie scorer in history.

Most points in a test match
In the Asian qualifier tournament for the 1995 World Cup, held in Kuala Lumpur, Malaysia, 22-29 October 1994, Hong Kong fullback Ashley Billington scored 10 tries for a total of 50 points! The unlucky victims were Singapore who suffered a world record defeat to the tune of 164-13 in the same game. In a World Cup game in South Africa in 1995, Simon Culhane scored 45 points (1 try, 20 conversions) for New Zealand in a record smashing 145-17 victory over Japan. This edged out the World Cup record established only a week previously by Gavin Hastings of Scotland.

Hastings scored 44 points against Ivory Coast in a then record breaking 89-0 victory. Hastings' tally included 4 tries, 2 penalties and 9 conversions.

The previous record was held by Didier Camberabero of France who scored 30 points for France against Zimbabwe in the 1987 World Cup. This feat was equalled by Rob Andrew for England against Canada in a test on December 10 1994. (Andrew scored 6 conversions and 6 penalty goals.) These two therefore tie for fourth place.

Oldest Rugby Club?

This is a feat claimed by DUFC, otherwise known as Trinity College Rugby Club, of the University of Dublin. They claim that they were established in 1834 but other sources put the date at 1854. This would make the Cambridge University club the oldest, as they were formed in 1839.

The first official Rugby Union club was Guy's Hospital Rugby Club (London, England), formed in 1843.

The World's Largest Rugby Club?

This distinction is claimed by Stellenbosch University in South Africa who boast several thousand players. It should be noted though that membership is compulsory for all resident students! Nevertheless they field at least 45 teams in an intra-club, residence-based, league, as well as the regular club teams.

Highest career total points in test matches

Michael Lynagh of Australia scored 911 career points before he retired from international rugby after the 1995 World Cup at the age of 31 and with 76 caps. His points total comprises 17 tries, 140 conversions, 177 penalties goals, 9 field goals.

Highest number of points scored in a test debut

Simon Culhane (of Southland), scored 45 points in his test debut for New Zealand, on 4 June, in a 145-17 drubbing of Japan at the 1995 World Cup. He scored one try, which he converted and converted 19 other tries (making 20 conversions altogether, another record). He only missed one shot at goal all day, a minor miss of the one remaining try in the All Black's tally. Interestingly, New Zealand had no penalty goal attempts in the entire match. Culhane's total was also a record individual score for a World Cup final series game and is the second highest individual score ever in an international match.

The same game also saw Marc Ellis, playing at centre, score a record 6 tries in a test for New Zealand. Not all of Culhane's kicks were easy. Several tries were out wide, and even into the sun, and towards the end of the match a couple of try scorers made little or no attempt to run their tries in behind the posts! This record on debut eclipsed the previous record set only a month earlier by Andrew Mehrtens. Mehrtens (of Canterbury), scored 28 points in his test debut for New Zealand against Canada in Auckland, April 22, 1995. His tally included a try (5), three penalty goals (9) and seven conversions (14) and was only two points short of the then third place world record test score.

New Zealand won the game 73-7 in what was Canada's heaviest defeat in an international. The game was a build-up for both sides prior to the 1995 World Cup. (Mehrtens was rested for the above World Cup pool game with Japan.) Prior to these two feats the previous record on debut had been 23 by Matthew Cooper, also of New Zealand.

Strange but True!
Scrum at the Whitehouse?

President Clinton is a former rugby player! He was introduced to the game while a Rhode's scholar at Oxford. His talents have been reputedly described as "By no means athletic, in fact a bit lumpy", but Clinton did play a bit as a second row forward. He also turned out for The Little Rock Rugby club in his home state of Arkansas.

Holy game?
Pope John Paul II was an accomplished rugby player. In fact he represented Poland at International level.

Healthy state of affairs?
Jonah Lomu is suing his insurance company over a sickness claim after he was sidelined with a kidney disease. He is taking GIO Insurance to court after they refused to accept his claim.

Made of money?
The Calcutta Cup (played for annually between England and Scotland) was made from the rupees when the Calcutta rugby club folded. Although the withdrawal of British troops from India caused its ultimate demise, the event that had previously lead to a dramatic reduction in its membership was the withdrawal of a free bar as a membership privilege!

Rugby dictator
Idi Amin (former leader of Uganda) was an official reserve for East Africa Vs the 1955 touring British Lions.

Black day for Uganda
Uganda turned out to play Kenya in Entebbe in 1935, but both sides had white shirts. A lady spectator eventually provided a large bottle of black dye, and using the water bucket they dyed their shirts black. They have played in black from then on.

Kicking hooker
Robert Thompson, a Maori, is unusual in being Western Australia's only international. He also had an unusual role as a goal-kicking hooker. He took up goal kicking to strengthen his leg following an injury.

Synchronised scrummage?
Although rugby is played in 135 countries, it was rejected from the 2004 Olympics because it was not considered a truly 'global sport'. It can only be assumed that rugby had to make way for other global sports, such as synchronised swimming!

Yew wooden believe it
Western Samoa's first international was against Fiji in 1924. The game kicked off at 7am so the Samoans could go to work afterwards. The match was played in a local park, and there was a tree in the centre of the pitch!

French farce
Andre Behoteguy played 19 Internationals between 1923 and 1929 while wearing a beret.

Don't get your hands dirty?
Basil McLear, who played for Ireland between 1905 and 1907, he did so in white gloves!

Eye see!
Dolway Walkington who represented Ireland between 1887 and 1891 wore a monocle on the pitch while playing, removing it just before making a tackle! Another famous 'eye man' was Joe Simpson who played for Wales in 1884. He actually played his Rugby while wearing glasses!

A to Z Of Rugby

A guide to some of the terms, used in the world of Rugby Union.

Advantage-line
This is the imaginary line that extends across the field from where the last scrum, ruck, maul, lineout or play the ball was formed. This is used as a measure of how much good has been done within the game and how good each side is.

Against the head
Describes the rare occurrence of the ball being hooked by the opposition after the scrummage put in.

All Blacks
The national team of New Zealand.

Backs
The group of players normally numbered 9 through 15 who do not participate in scrums and line-outs, except for the scrum-half.

Barbarians
The name of invitational rugby teams, the most famous based in the UK, drawing the finest players from around the world together to play matches against international teams. Also called the BaaBaas.

Binding
The careful method players grip and grasp each other to form a secure scrum, ruck, or maul. This is a critical skill to ensure the safety of players.

Bledisloe Cup
The annual competition between the national teams of New Zealand and Australia. Now held during the Tri-Nations Competition.

Bomb
A high kick into the air designed to usually put pressure on the opposition fullback. This pressure comes from the chasers who try to reclaim the ball or at least take out the fullback.

Calcutta Cup
The annual match between England and Scotland each year during the 5 Nations tournament. The trophy is made from the coins remaining after the Calcutta Rugby Club disbanded in the Twenties.

Cap
Anytime a player plays in a match he/she is technically awarded a cap but the term is mostly used to note the number of official games a player has appeared for His national team against another national team. A cap is an honour, there is typically no physical item awarded.

Cardiff Arms Park
The home stadium of the national team of Wales in Cardiff, Wales.

Centre
Either of the backs wearing number 12 (inside) or number 13 (outside). Powerful runners they are the heart of the back running attack and defence. The inside centre can also be called the 2nd 5/8th.

Charge Down
The blocking of a kick by an opposition's player.

Clearing Kick
A kick of the ball to touch which relieves pressure on a side under heavy attack by the opposition.

Collapsing the Scrum
When a scrum goes to ground (i.e. the front rows tumble to the floor) it is said to have collapsed. This is often used as a spoiling tactic and can be penalised by penalties or even penalty tries.

Conversion Kick
A kick at the posts after the awarding of a try scoring two points if successful. The kick must be attempted directly from a spot perpendicular to the spot where the try was awarded. Usually taken with a place kick, it can be rushed when the kicker makes a move towards the ball.

A TO Z OF RUGBY

Dead
The ball is for the time being out of play. This occurs when the referee blows his whistle to indicate a stoppage of play or when an attempt to convert a try is unsuccessful.

Defending Team
The team in whose half of the ground the stoppage of play occurs and the opponents of the defending team are referred to as 'the Attacking Team'.

Drop Goal
A kick at the posts taken at anytime a side is close to their own try line. If successful it scores three points but the ball must hit the ground before being kicked.

Eagles
The national team of the United States of America.

Ellis, William Webb
The person, as a student at Rugby School, credited with inspiring the modern game of rugby football in 1823. He later became a priest and passed away in Southern France.

Feed
The rolling of the ball into the scrum by the scrum-half. Must be straight down the tunnel.

Fifteens
The name of the most common game of rugby union featuring fifteen total players per side. Each team consists of eight forwards and seven backs playing two halves each 40 minutes long.

50-50 ball
Any ball that can be contested by either side is said to be 50 - 50, especially in the case of up and unders or in some line-outs.

Five Nations
The annual tournament from January through March between the national men's teams of England, Wales, Scotland, Ireland, and France.

Flanker
Either of the two forwards wearing number 6 or number 7. Also called wing forwards or breakaways they bind to the scrum outside of the locks just behind the outside hip of the props. They can play always on the same side of the scrum or can specialise on either the weak-side or strong-side. The players with the fewest set responsibilities, their job is to aggressively pursue the ball, gain possession, and take off running.

Flyhalf
The back wearing number 10 who normally receives the ball from the scrum-half. Also called the Out-half, Outside half or 1st 5/8th, he will call plays for the back-line, pass the ball to other backs, or provide most of the tactical kicks.

Forward Pass
An illegal pass to a player ahead of the ball causing the ball to be awarded to the other team in a scrum.

Forwards
The group of players normally numbered 1 through 8 who bind together into scrums, line-up for line-outs, and commit themselves to most rucks and mauls.

Free Kick
A uncontested kick awarded to a team usually for a minor penalty by the other team. The kick cannot be taken directly at the posts except by a drop goal.

Front Row
The common name for the Prop/Hooker/Prop combination at the front of a scrum.

Fullback
The back wearing number 15 who normally plays deep behind the back-line. In offence the fullback is a dangerous attacking position hitting holes unexpectedly at pace, in defence the fullback has the primary responsibility for covering all tactical kicks down field by the opposition.

A TO Z OF RUGBY

Grand Slam
A Five Nations championship won without any losses or draws.

Grubber
A kick of the ball which cause the ball to bounce and roll along the ground.

Haka
A cultural ceremony display with a chant performed by many Southern Pacific teams as a challenge before a match at the centre of the pitch.

High Ball
Ball kicked very high into the air placing any player attempting to catch it under extreme pressure by on rushing opposition players.

Home Nations
England, Wales, Scotland, and Ireland.

Hooker
The front-row forward wearing number 2. The player is supported on either side in the scrum by props and is required to gain possession of the ball in the scrum by hooking or blocking the ball with one of His feet. The hooker will normally also be the forward throwing the ball into the lineout.

Injury Time
During a half, the clock is stopped by the referee while any injury is attended to. After the normal half's time has expired (eg forty minutes) the continued play afterwards equal to the amount of injury stoppage is called injury time.

IRFB
The International Rugby Football Board. The IRFB is the ruling body for Rugby Union world-wide and has primary responsibility for setting and adjusting the laws of the sport and running the Rugby World Cup championships for 15s and 7s every four years.

Jumper
A common name for a rugby jersey. Also the name of a player in a

lineout, usually at the 2,4, and 6 positions, jumping to catch or intercept the throw.

Knock On
Losing, dropping, or knocking the ball forward from a player's hand resulting in the ball being awarded to the other team in a scrum.

Knock Forward
Same as Knock On.

Lansdowne Road
The home stadium of the Irish national team in Dublin, Ireland.

League
S version of rugby played normally with thirteen players under different laws than Rugby Union. The two codes deviated over professionalism and are usually contentious towards each other.

Leg Up
An offence where a hooker brings his foot into the scrum's tunnel before the ball is fed by the scrum-half.

Lifting
The act of lifting the lineout jumper into the air in order to more easily catch or intercept the throw.

Line-out
The set-play restarting play after the ball has been taken out or kicked to touch. Both sets of forwards will line up opposite each other with the side with throw calling a play. The throw must be directly down the middle of the two lines.

Lock
Either of the two forwards normally wearing No. 4 and No. 5. Typically the largest players on the field, they have primary responsibility for being the power in scrums and securing the ball in line-outs. Due to their size, they are also normally powerful forces in all loose play, rucks, and mauls.

A TO Z OF RUGBY

Loose-head
The No. 1 prop in a scrum due to his head being outside the opposition's tight-head prop's shoulders.

Loose Forwards
Common names for the flankers and number 8 in a forward pack.

Mark
A location on the pitch designated by the referee as the location a scrum should come together. Also a word a player will call while catching a kicked ball within his own 22 meter line. If awarded by the referee, that back is awarded a free kick.

Maul
Typically after a runner has come into contact and the ball is still being held by a player once any combination of at least three players have bound themselves a maul has been set. The primary difference from a ruck is that the ball is not on the ground.

Milking
A player will quite often will pretend to be interfered with in the play the ball or a half back may throw a dummy pass in order to receive a penalty from the referee, such a tactic is known as milking.

Melrose Cup
The trophy awarded the champions of the Rugby World Cup 7s. Currently held by Fiji.

Murrayfield
The home stadium of the national team of Scotland in Edinburgh, Scotland.

Number 8
The forward who wears the jersey with the number 8. This player binds into the scrum normally at the very base between the two locks. His responsibility is to initiate attacks by the forwards from scrums or to provide a stable ball from the scrum for the scrum-half.

Off-sides
During rucks, scrums, line-outs, and mauls an imaginary line is present over which any player crossing before the set piece is completed commits a penalty.

Outside Centre
The back wearing number 13.

Pack
Another name for all the forwards usually when they are bound for a scrum.

PacRim or Pacific Rim
The annual spring tournament between the national teams of the USA, Canada, Hong Kong, and Japan.

Penalty
Any number of infractions or violations which award the other team a kick.

Penalty Kick
An uncontested kick awarded to a team for a major infraction by the other team. The kick can be taken directly at goal and scores 3 points if successful. If the ball is kicked to touch, then the ball is awarded back to the team which kicked the ball out of bounds.

Penalty Try
The awarding of a try due to a flagrant violation by an opposing side that prevents an obvious try from being scored.

Place Kick
A kick of the ball resting on the ground, placed in an indention in the ground, from a small pile of sand, or from a kicking tee. Place kicks are used to start each half, for penalty kicks at goal, or for conversion kicks after a try has been awarded.

Pop Kick
A short shallow kick usually delivered over the head of an onrushing

A TO Z OF RUGBY

defender to be quickly retrieved or caught by the kicker or one of His supporting players.

Prop
Either of the two forwards normally wearing number 1 (loose-head) or number 3 (tight-head). Responsibilities are to support the hooker during scrums and 2nd rows during line-outs.

Pumas
The national team of Argentina.

Punt
Made by letting the ball fall from the hand (or hands) and kicking it before it touches the ground.

Pushover Try
A try scored by the forward pack as a unit in a scrum-down by pushing the opposition's scrum pack backwards across the try-line while dragging the ball underneath them. Typically scored from a five metre scrum, the try is usually awarded when the number 8 or scrum-half touch the ball down after it crosses the try line

Ranfurly Shield
A challenge trophy between the provincial sides of New Zealand.

Referee
The sole judge and timekeeper of the game.

Restart
The kick restarting play after a half or after points are scored.

Ruck
Typically after a runner has come into contact and the ball has been delivered to the ground once any combination of at least three players have bound themselves a ruck has been set. The primary difference from a maul is that the ball is on the ground.

RWC
Short for Rugby World Cup. Tournaments played every four years for

Men's 15s, Women's 15s, Men's 7s, U-21 men, and U-19 men.

Rugger
Another name for a rugby player or the game of Rugby, either Union or League.

SANZAR
Tournament involving South Africa, New Zealand and Australia.

Scrum
The formation used in the set-play restarting play after a knock-on or forward pass. The forwards from each side bind together and then the two packs come together to allow the scrum-half with the feed to deliver the ball to the scrum. A scrum can also be awarded or chosen in different circumstances by the referee.

Scrum-down
The coming together of the scrum.

Scrum-half
The back wearing number 9 who normally feeds the ball into a scrum and retrieves the ball at the base of scrums, rucks, and mauls. Can also be called the halfback.

Scrummaging
The process of setting and completing a scrum

Second Row
Another name for the two locks in a forward pack.

Selection
The process of picking a squad for a match by a club or team. Also an identifier of a player selected to play a match.

Selector
A person involved in the selection process.

Send-off
After flagrant, numerous or a malicious foul, the referee can elect to expel

A TO Z OF RUGBY

a player from the match. The player cannot be replaced causing the side to play one person short. Normally the sent off player is banned for at least one match after the send-off and depending on the severity of the offence can be banned for more than one match to life.

Sevens
A form of rugby union invented in Scotland and played with only seven total players, usually three forwards and four backs. Each half typically last only 7 minutes but can be longer. Games are almost always played during tournaments.

Springboks
The national team of South Africa.

Stomping
When rucking gets dangerous, ie if a boot is being raked across the head of another player, it is called stomping.

Super Twelve
The annual tournament between the best provincial teams of Australia, New Zealand, and South Africa.

Take
A well executed catch of a kicked ball.

Tens
a form of rugby union played with only ten total players. Each half typically last only 10 minutes but can be longer. Games are almost always played during tournaments.

Ten Metres
The distance which the defending team must stand back from the play the ball.

Test
The name typically used for matches between two national teams. The match can also be called an international.

Tight Five
A common name for all of the front (props and hooker) and second row (locks) forwards.

Tight-head
The number 3 prop in a scrum due to his head being between the opposition's hooker and loose-head prop's shoulders. A scrum can also win a tight-head by taking possession of the ball in a scrum fed by the other pack.

Touch, touchline
The out of bounds line that runs on either side of the pitch. The non-contact version of rugby is also commonly called touch.

Touch Judge
An official posted on each side of the pitch to mark the spot where balls go out of touch and to judge kicks at goal. The touch judge is also instrumental in pointing out any serious violence infractions not seen by the referee.

Tour
A trip by a club or team typically to a foreign country playing a number of different matches.

TriNations
The annual competition between the national men's teams of Australia, New Zealand, and South Africa.

Try
A score of 5 points awarded when the ball is carried or kicked across the try-line and touched down to the ground by a player.

Try-line
The goal line extending across the pitch.

Tunnel
The gap between the front rows in a scrum or the gap between the two lines of forwards in a lineout.

A TO Z OF RUGBY

22 Meter Dropout
The kick which restarts play after a missed penalty or drop goal passing the end goal line or touched down by a defending player. The ball is kicked back to the original attacking side.

Twickenham
The home stadium of the national team of England in Twickenham, England.

U19
Players under the age of 19.

U21
Players under the age of 21.

Union
Another name for the most popular form of rugby featuring either 15, 10, or 7 players per side. The local, provincial, or national organising body for rugby competition is also often called a union.

USARFU
The United States of America Rugby Football Union.

Up and under
A tactical kick which is popped very high and shallow allowing the kicker and supporting players to easily run underneath it for recovery. The kick is intended to put heavy pressure on any opposition player attempting to catch the ball. Also called a Garryowen due to the Irish club which originated the play.

Wallabies
The national team of Australia.

Weak-side
From a set piece, ruck or maul, the short side of the field. Also called the blindside.

William Webb Ellis Trophy
The trophy awarded the Men's champions of the Rugby World Cup 15s.

Currently held by South Africa.

Wing forward
another term for a Flanker.

Winger
Either of the two backs wearing No. 11 or No. 14. Each will normally stay on the same side of the back line they are on throughout the match and are typically expected to be the fastest sprinters in the side. Wingers also have key duties during defence helping the fullback cover kicks and counterattacking.

XV
A common identifier for the first fifteen selected players of a club or team. A team can also use XV in their name, pronounced as fifteen.

Zinzan
A drop-goal attempt from 40-50 metres by a forward which only gets about 2-3m off the deck. Named after the couple of efforts Zinzan Brooke tried in the 1994 All Black Vs South Africa tests.